The
Honeymoon
Handbook

The Honeymoon Handbook

A GUIDE TO LIFE'S

MOST ROMANTIC ADVENTURE

Marcia Powell & Lynn Graeme

MACMILLAN PUBLISHING CO., INC.

NEW YORK

COLLIER MACMILLAN PUBLISHERS

LONDON

Macmillan Publishing Co., Inc.
866 Third Avenue, New York, N.Y. 10022
Collier Macmillan Canada, Ltd.

Library of Congress Cataloging in Publication Data
Powell, Marcia.
The honeymoon handbook.
Includes index.
1. Travel etiquette. 2. Honeymoon.
I. Graeme, Lynn, joint author. II. Title.
BJ2156.H6P68   646.7'8   80–19942
ISBN 0–02–598520–5

10 9 8 7 6 5 4 3 2 1

Designed by Jack Meserole

Printed in the United States of America

To those special men
who believe in
fantasy, romance,
and dreams

CONTENTS

Section One
PLANNING YOUR JOURNEY

Section Two
PREPARING FOR THE JOURNEY

CONTENTS

Section Three
ON THE JOURNEY

Section Four
TO SMOOTH THE JOURNEY

Section Five
NUTS AND BOLTS

ACKNOWLEDGMENTS

Dreams seldom become reality without the efforts of many people, and *The Honeymoon Handbook* is no exception. We are deeply grateful to the friends, colleagues, and associates who aided and encouraged us in this project.

To list all those who assisted us would take another book; however, there are several special people whom we want to recognize. Without Michael M. Smith, *The Honeymoon Handbook* would not have been possible. From the conception, in which he played the major role, through the planning, research, writing, and manuscript production, Michael directed every phase of this project. Above all, he believed.

Jean Rodgers lent her invaluable professional skills to almost every aspect of the book—research, writing, and focus. Lenore Street and Suzanne M. Henry, who assisted with research, and Helen Kessler, our typist, had the patience of a saint. With her impeccable sense of structure and enthusiastic support, our editor Joyce Jack guided us through the publishing labyrinth.

Our very special friends Daniel Piliero, Dennis O'Neil, and Rica Martens Smith stood by us and propped us up when our energy and aspirations were fading.

To these people and all the others—particularly those who shared with us their own honeymoon experiences—we offer our sincere appreciation.

PREFACE

There has never been a book exactly like this—one volume that covers the honeymoon journey emotionally, physically, and geographically.

A map is not a journey—it can only show the lay of the land, locate points of interest, and warn of dangers. Just so, this book is a sort of map. In it we've collected and made the best sense possible of the honeymoon experiences of ourselves and literally hundreds of others. Nevertheless, your honeymoon will be uniquely yours.

Because a honeymoon is so many diverse things—a spiritual retreat, a sexual awakening, a vacation, and a magical ceremony —our tone changes according to what aspect of the wedding journey is being considered.

In Sections One through Four, the chapters emphasize the emotional and sexual aspects of the honeymoon, so they tend to be more lyrical. In Section Five, the "practical" chapters listing many useful resources—books, addresses, information—chug along on short, workaday words and phrases. The content (what's being discussed) decides the form (how something is said). After all, feathers and hammers are both necessary—and desirable—but not for the same jobs.

Use this book as both a friend and a tool. Write in the margins, underline, and use the charts and graphs. Jot down your comments in the blank spaces. Make this book personally *yours,* just as your honeymoon will be.

A honeymoon is:

. . . a tradition
. . . a relaxing period of adjustment to being married
. . . a symbolic breaking away from the family
. . . a chance for intimacy before returning to the "rat race"
. . . a chance to get to know one another
. . . a means of relaxing and recovering from the hectic activities of the marriage planning and ceremony
. . . a chance to establish yourselves as a new family unit
. . . a starting point

INTRODUCTION:

HONEYMOON MAGIC

REGARDLESS of your reasons for taking a wedding trip, your honeymoon should be what you want it to be so it will cast a glow over the whole beginning of your marriage—an aura of happiness that will stay with you all your lives. In this book we'll be helping you plan your honeymoon from beginning to end, helping you to investigate possibilities and narrow down options. Your honeymoon is important and you are the only experts when it comes to what you want.

Although many other traditions have faded away, the honeymoon remains—stronger than ever. Cutting across religious barriers and including every economic class, it's enjoyed by the young and the not-so-young. The reason the honeymoon tradition lives on is that it fulfills so many needs and desires. Yet it began in most cultures as a sort of preventive magic.

Ancient peoples believed themselves to be surrounded by spirits who had to be both appeased and outwitted. The newlyweds—particularly the bride—were thought to be particularly vulnerable to the outrages of mischievous spirits because of their innocence and happiness.

The custom of carrying the bride over the threshold came about because it was thought that jealous spirits would try to trip her as she entered her new home for the first time, bringing her bad luck. Rice was thrown at a wedding to assure prosperity for the couple. Noisy objects were often tied to the getaway vehicle (which often wasn't a vehicle at all but a mule or horse) in order to frighten away minor demons who might try to follow the newlyweds home. The reasons behind some other marriage and honeymoon customs have been forgotten, but modern newlyweds seem to enjoy following them just the same.

It might be fun to observe a few modern variations of ancient honeymoon customs and magic charms. The Chinese, for instance, hang three long strips of red paper with good wishes written on them over the nuptial bed and cover the bed itself with red cloths. You could do the same, writing down your own wishes—serious or funny—and covering the bed with red satin sheets. Another Chinese custom is to burn two large red candles throughout the wedding night—think of the beautiful glow that red streamers, red satin sheets, and candles would cast over your first honeymoon night! Bermudian newlyweds plant a small tree on the day they're married, so that it grows with their marriage. You could do the same.

More important than superstitions, though, is the symbolic gesture of the couple's breaking away from their families and creating a new family unit for themselves. The marriage ceremony legally makes a couple husband and wife, but it takes everyone a little while to get used to the idea. This is one of the important reasons why honeymoons have always been so popular. As one bridegroom said, "It's important for a couple to go away— to symbolize the fact that they'll be spending their lives together. Even if the couple has been living together, the honeymoon is a chance to establish the marriage relationship."

The honeymoon is also just a great time to kick up your heels and have fun before settling down—to see new places, meet new people, and try new things. When we interviewed honeymooners we asked them what they remembered most about their honeymoon. Some of the answers:

"It was fantastic! Nothing to do but enjoy the beautiful beach and let the tension flow out of us. . . ."

"The pleasure of being together, carefree, doing things as one. . . ."

"The wonderful experiences we shared together . . . relaxing, enjoying, seeing some sensational places together for the first time."

"Joy."

A honeymoon is important in beginning a marriage well, although lack of one certainly doesn't doom a couple to marital unhappiness. Still, a honeymoon is a once-in-a-marriage opportunity, a celebration of yourselves and your love for one another.

Some of the couples we interviewed who hadn't been able to take an immediate after-the-wedding honeymoon spoke of the letdown and sense of insignificance that the lack of a honeymoon had cast on their marriage. Said one woman, "We got married Saturday, and Monday we were both back in our offices. If someone had asked, 'What did you do over the weekend?' we would've answered, 'Oh, nothing much. We just got married.'"

It apparently isn't important that your wedding journey be long, either in distance or time. What is important is that you get away from your friends and families and accustomed surroundings, if only for a day or two. This might be accomplished by borrowing the apartment or beach house of a friend, or by going to a hotel or motel. Just a short amount of time spent alone together, perhaps with some champagne, flowers in the room, and loving feelings can be enough to create a delicious, romantic mood.

This warm and wonderful romantic feeling is the kind of magic we associate with the honeymoon experience. With the opportunity to concentrate on each other and on your love for one another, you'll find your senses become more acute. Colors, sounds, and sensations are all intensely new. Experiences that might seem ordinary at other times catch the glow and become extraordinary. Because of this heightened feeling, events that happen during your honeymoon are remembered for many, many years.

Indeed, probably your whole life long.

And that is magical in itself.

Section One

PLANNING YOUR JOURNEY

1. PLANNING YOUR HONEYMOON

HONEYMOONERS today are perhaps the most fortunate in history. You have your choice of all the world's beautiful places, some of which would have been impractical or even unreachable only fifty years ago. With so many diverse options available, there's probably no couple who can't find a honeymoon to suit them.

Without knowing you, we couldn't tell you what honeymoon choice would be best for you—and wouldn't even if we could. Part of the excitement of the honeymoon is in finding out about different places, discussing them, making your choice, and then watching your plans fall into place and your dreams come true.

Planning a honeymoon is fun!

To get you started thinking of ideas, here are a few categories of honeymoon travel you might want to consider:

The Traditional Honeymoon

Hotels, inns, guesthouses, and resorts make excellent honeymoon spots. They provide you with as much privacy as you want, plus good food and service.

A **hotel** room can become a romantic world of your own. A candlelit dinner, champagne breakfast in bed, flowers all around . . . all these as well as many other services are yours while you relax and love in delicious privacy. No chores, no responsibilities—just peace.

If your hotel is in a city, you can venture out at will to sample urban delights: plays, museums, and fine restaurants. If it rains or snows, you still have a wide choice of things to do. In fact, walking down city streets beneath a shared umbrella with the rain falling around you can be an incredibly romantic experience. You can sleep all day if you like with the city humming around you, and waiters, maids, and management there to satisfy your requests. If they are notified ahead of time that you're honeymooners, most hotels will provide some extras such as flowers in the room or a bottle of wine or champagne. Some hotels offer special weekend or week-long rates, including such treats as champagne breakfasts in bed.

You needn't travel far. Almost everyone lives within a short distance of a good hotel, probably in a large city. You can enjoy a change of scene, service, and the privacy needed for romance close to your home.

Inns. If you want to awaken to the sound of birds fluttering in the trees and begin each day with a good hearty country breakfast, look into inns. Inns can be found in cities, in small towns, or in the country. Look for one that has been declared a national landmark, and enjoy spending your honeymoon in an antique bed in a room that may have housed Alexander Hamilton or Edgar Allan Poe. If possible, get a room with a fireplace so you can enjoy private dinners and gaze into the flames together.

Guesthouses. Even more homey than inns are guesthouses. Most contain no more than twelve rooms, usually far fewer. They are much less expensive, on the whole, than either hotels or inns. The atmosphere in guesthouses varies as much as the hosts. Some create a family feeling, while others are more impersonal. Like inns, guesthouses are sometimes historical landmarks and usually were once huge old family homes. The sole disadvantage to guesthousing is that you probably won't have a private bathroom.

Renting. The ultimate combination of privacy and service luxury might be to rent an apartment or house, complete with servants. Renting a place in a vacation area, even with servants and plush surroundings, needn't be impossibly expensive, especially if you're honeymooning fairly close to home. In fact, it might be no more expensive than a good hotel. If you've always wanted to live like a millionaire, this may be your chance!

Resorts. In some ways, resorts are the way you wished summer camps had been when you were a child—no counselors to tell you what to do, but social directors to offer you choices; good food; comfortable rooms; entertainment; and no "lights out." During the day you can take part in the many activities and sports most resorts offer or just loaf on the beach or patio. Then, after a delicious dinner either in the dining room or in the privacy of your room, you can go dancing in the resort night club.

What are some of the activities resorts offer? Sailing, boating, water and winter skiing, horseback riding, tennis, golf, swimming, bowling, exercise classes, dance lessons, archery . . . and on and on. It is well-nigh impossible to be bored at a resort. But if privacy is what you want, you can also have that. There's no obligation to take part in any activity. As with hotels, if the resort management knows you're honeymooners, it's likely to offer some extra luxuries at no charge.

The **honeymoon resort** is an exciting and astonishingly inexpensive variation. At these resorts there are no children, no families—just couples beginning their lives together. Since everyone else is a honeymooner too, you won't feel "strange" or conspicuous. You can be openly romantic and indulge in talk about your wedding.

The decor at these resorts is romantic and luxurious in the extreme. Extra-large beds and baths (both sometimes heart-shaped), plush carpeting, seemingly *acres* of mirrors, and color television are standard equipment. In deluxe suites you can expect to find his-and-her bathrooms, fireplaces, and even your own private indoor pool! Honeymoon resorts offer the same—or more—activities as other resorts, as well as special games, parties, and get-acquainted functions planned especially for honeymooners.

A Kid at Heart

For most of us, thoughts of romance probably conjure up candlelight, soft music, and flowers . . . and these are a vital, traditional aspect of the honeymoon. But they don't have to be the whole honeymoon. Suppose that what you'd really like is a chance to throw off all responsibility and regain your childlike love of sheer *fun?*

One young couple decided to do just that:

"We got tired of being grown-ups," explained Kathy, a twenty-year-old student from Akron. "It was exciting getting ready for the wedding and all that, but hectic, too. And we realized we had a couple of tough years coming up with my being in school and Jim trying to get ahead in the accounting firm where he works. One day we were talking and it came out that we'd both wanted to go to one of these huge *amusement parks—* you know, the ones that cover *acres—*when we were kids, but hadn't. We looked at each other and said, 'Why not? Why not spend our honeymoon at a giant amusement park and just be two kids on a great spree with no adults around to spoil the fun?' And it was *great!*"

So if the two of you would like an early second childhood, think about the things you wanted to do as a kid, or even did do, that you'd like to do on your honeymoon. If you always had a secret yen to be Dale Evans or the Lone Ranger, you can honeymoon at a dude ranch with horses galore and enjoy good plain grub from cookouts under a western sky. If you'd like to get back in touch with "the simple life," you can stay at one of the farms across the country that accept paying guests.

After all, there's plenty of time for romance late at night and early in the morning when your suite or room or pup tent is your own cozy nest.

Going Mobile

Is there a gypsy in your soul? If the idea of wandering together over the nation's highways appeals to you, it can be done. You can follow a coastline or historic trails or just your whims. Here's how:

Motor homes are basically small apartments on wheels. They range in size and style from seventeen-foot campers to palatial thirty-two-foot models that rival most hotel rooms. The driver sits at the wheel within the motor home itself, so that he or she isn't isolated. You have a bedroom, kitchen, and bathroom—all the comforts of home, but on wheels. The cost of renting a motor home is comparable to the cost of staying in a hotel for the same length of time. You must, however, figure in the cost and accessibility of gasoline and oil. One couple in their fifties, enjoying a "fifth honeymoon," rented a motor home and drove through Nevada and Arizona, stopping for days at a time when the fishing was good and enjoying candlelit dinners in their motor-home dining room.

Using a *trailer* for your mobile honeymoon requires a little more planning and roughing it, since they aren't entirely self-contained units like motor homes. They do, however, have sleeping space, kitchen space, toilet, and shower. They're less expensive to rent than motor homes and have the advantage of being lighter to pull. There's no special license required to drive either a motor home or a trailer. To find companies that rent either or both, look in the Yellow Pages under "Motor Homes—Renting and Leasing."

If you're interested in *pitching a tent* along the way, your car can be your mobile honeymoon headquarters. Just be sure to have reservations at the trailer and camping parks where you expect to stop. *You'll need reservations*, especially during the summer. However, you can also camp alongside some rivers or lakes in delicious privacy. Just be sure to find out to whom the property belongs and ask before you make yourself at home. Promise to "police" the area before you leave.

Are *motorcycles* romantic? Two on a cycle certainly calls for closeness, and whizzing down the road with the air whipping around you is exhilarating. So if you want to make your honeymoon trip a *trip*, this might be one way. You can stop at motels or, if both of you ride and you use two motorcycles, you'll have space to carry a tent and other supplies. Unconventional? Yes! But it might be just what you'd like.

In Europe, young people often take long trips by *bicycle*, either carrying backpacks and bundles on the back for camping, or staying at hostels, inns, or hotels along the way. If you have time and the countryside is pleasant to travel through, this could be a lovely experience.

Bus companies offer trips of anywhere from two days' to three weeks' duration at very low prices. These package prices include transportation, accommodations, and entrance to entertainment facilities (usually), as well as some meals. Since the trips are taken in a motor coach with its well-padded seats and bathroom on board, air conditioning, and often music, this is a pleasant way to visit a popular area or place. You can lean back in comfort, talk, hold hands, play backgammon, chess, or word games, and see the country close up.

The Call of the Wild

If you've ever heard the sighing sound of a lush evergreen forest and felt the earth and pine needles beneath your feet, you've experienced romance. It's the most ancient and basic kind of romance—close to the earth, mysterious, and ageless. Imagine walking through peaceful woods, bathing in streams or spring-fed lakes, and sitting alone together by a fire before going inside your tent to cuddle together with the soothing whisper of wind-blown trees to sing you to sleep.

And you don't need much—some basic camping skills, a forest, a minimum of gear (some of which can be rented), and good companionship.

So popular have *camping and backpacking* become that you'll need to make reservations for visiting your national or state forest of choice. Write to the forest management six months ahead for reservations and information about any fees, regulations, or advice on using the facility.

If your budget and ambitions are both large, you can stay at a *hunting and/or fishing lodge.* Some of these have food that compares well with that at many resorts or hotels, as well as other activities besides hunting and fishing. Whether you choose to lodge in the state where you live or in the middle of the Alaskan wilderness where you have to be flown in by amphibious plane, a good lodge is sure to provide hearty food, activity, new friends, and a delicious respite from civilization.

The Lure of the Sea

Scientists say we all originally came from the sea—isn't it time you went home for a visit? Out on the ocean, salt-laden breezes refresh you. Blue waters flashing with sunlight or rippling with moonlight are framed by the huge, curving, downturned bowl of the sky. Legend has it that walking along the deck of a ship with a member of the opposite sex inspires madly passionate love—how much more effective with people who are already in love!

A favorite way to enjoy the magical romance of the ocean is the *cruise,* and no wonder. A cruise ship is a floating hotel with food, parties, dancing, movies, sports, swimming, card playing, and an almost endless assortment of other activities. On board: a flotilla of people dedicated to enjoying themselves thoroughly. For a honeymooner, it can be a paradise. You can have privacy and comfort, company and recreation, in the amounts *you* want, all presided over by a conscientious staff and the magic of the sea.

Another way to spend a honeymoon at sea is to sign up for a cruise aboard a *sailing ship.* On this sort of voyage, you set sail with a group but enjoy your own cabin. You're encouraged to take part in sailing the ship, but not pressed to do so.

These cruises are a bargain. One prepaid price covers everything (except tips and shopping sprees) and compares well with the same level of accommodations on land. Just be sure to have your travel agent check on the clientele of any cruise in which you're interested, to make certain that you aren't surrounded by people with whom you don't have much in common.

Then there are *beach and island resorts* that offer the expected resort luxuries plus such aquatic pleasures as sailing, scuba, and skin diving. Lessons and equipment are available so even novices can explore the lovely and fantastic coral reefs.

The ocean suggests mystery and romance—both surely appropriate for a honeymoon.

Faraway Places

Have you ever imagined yourselves strolling hand in hand down sunlit Italian streets, skiing down a Swiss slope, or dining in the grand hall of a three-hundred-year-old castle in Germany? Going abroad needn't be outrageously expensive, and some of the ways to hold costs down will actually *add* to the enjoyment and romance of your trip.

It's least expensive to go abroad if you plan to stay in one place the entire time. You'll get to know the people and the place on a one-to-one basis, not through the glass window of a tour bus.

Cost is reduced and pleasure doubled when you stay in a venerable or even historic inn or guesthouse abroad, rather than a hotel. You'll enjoy meals *en famille* when you don't choose to dine alone in your room. You'll make real friends, rather than just acquaintances.

You'll save money if you "go native." Rent a house or an apartment for one to three weeks; it'll usually cost less than staying in a hotel. Buy your food where the locals do; drink what they drink with their meals. If the national drink is wine, have that; if beer, have *that*. And use public transportation whenever you can.

Tours may be fun and interesting, but they aren't always romantic. One young couple embarked on a three-week tour through Europe with a group of older, experienced travelers who were avid sightseers. Not only did the honeymooners feel out of place because of the age and interest differences between themselves and their companions, but the nonstop touring left them tired a great deal of the time. If you're sure you want a tour, have your travel agent match you up with a group that's close to you in age and interests.

When you're gathering information, you'll find that the national tourist bureau of the country you're interested in will supply more than enough information for starters. Just drop them a note.

Special-Interest Honeymoons

What do the two of you like so much that you think you could happily spend the rest of your life doing it? Sunbathing? Playing bridge? Cooking?

Whatever it is, you can build your honeymoon around it and have a marvelous time. It's easy to plan your own special-interest honeymoon. For instance, if you'd like an ocean cruise, you can find a company that offers theme tours. Among those that have been available recently are tours based on backgammon, football, cooking, old movies, detective stories, arts and crafts, horticulture, and the civilization of ancient Greece.

There are companies that will take you on trips down the Nile or Amazon rivers, on fishing expeditions in the wilds of Alaska or South America, and people who'll take you on photography trips through Africa, the American West, or even to the North and South poles!

Theme or special-interest honeymoons don't have to cost more than others. Many are arranged by scientific or other nonprofit societies and, in the case of theme cruises, you can enjoy the wonders of shipboard life in addition to the theme events at the usual cost for cruises.

Whatever your interest, mention it when talking with a travel agent, writing a tourist bureau, or making arrangements with an airline. What you might consider to be a most unlikely source of information about your favorite activity may prove to be a bonanza; for instance, some southern states have ski trails, and more than eighty-five train stations in France rent bicycles.

One couple said of their honeymoon, which was organized around their interest in anthropology, "It sounds kind of crazy, but we went to Peru and spent almost every day for three weeks digging while weird insects bit us. But it was exactly what we wanted and we loved it. And it wasn't all sweat and insect repellent. At night we could look out over the town from our balcony and listen to strange birds calling out and see about a million stars. . . ."

Honeymoon Magic

we went armed
with our sense of humor
we went equipped
with our sensible shoes
we went expecting
nothing tremendous—
just your typical
honeymoon

but the moon and stars
formed a conspiracy
the musing wind
hummed a tune
and to our surprise
we became romantics—
something we'd sworn
we'd never do!

so do beware
you sensible people
and cynics and you
with your feet on the ground:
through honeymoon magic
you'll lose your senses
and marvel and wonder
at what you've found!

2. ROMANTIC TRAVEL POSSIBILITIES: HOW TO CHOOSE?

THE LAST CHAPTER was meant to give you an idea of the many diverse possibilities for romantic honeymoon travel. How do you zero in on the honeymoon that is right for you?

Gather information: Begin at least three—but preferably six—months ahead by investigating every place you think you might be interested in visiting. Write to local, state, or national tourist bureaus or particular hotels or resorts that have attracted your attention (see the form letters in the back of this book).

When dealing with tourist bureaus, it's wise to remember that you'll get better service if you contact them during off-peak times. April through June are the busiest months for most offices, although the bureaus for the Caribbean islands and other warm-weather resort spots will be busier in the fall and winter.

If you're visiting the office in person, do it before 11 A.M. or after 3 P.M. The people who work in these offices take lunch hours too, so the offices are apt to be understaffed just when the lunchtime hordes descend.

If you're making your inquiries by telephone or mail, be as specific as possible. If need be, do a little research at the public library before writing or calling.

While you're waiting for brochures and other information to arrive, take out books from the library about places or subjects having to do with your honeymoon. Also, read newspaper and magazine travel features, plus travel and bride's magazines. Talk with friends and relatives about their honeymoon experiences and ask them for recommendations.

Once brochures begin to arrive, you'll probably feel pulled first toward one choice and then another as so many colorful and marvelous options are laid before you. There are ways to sift through all this material and zero in on the two or three honeymoon plans that will be right for you.

Budget. This must be the first consideration for most of us. Decide (and write down in a honeymoon planning notebook) what your entire honeymoon budget will be. If, as with most of us, you don't have an unlimited amount to spend, you'll have to make choices, so discuss and decide what's important to you. Would you prefer a weekend of carefree luxury or a longer time in more modest accommodations? Remember that you must include in your budget such extras as photographers, entertainment, gifts for friends and family, souvenirs for yourselves, transportation costs (cabs, rented car, gas, bus, train or plane tickets), tips, and emergencies.

One newlywed advised: "Plan to spend what you both feel you can afford and settle that ahead of time so you won't run into conflicts—also decide what you'll spend the money *on*." Once you arrive at your honeymoon place, be sure to consult one another about purchases. One couple went about blithely using their credit cards. Neither of them bought anything that was unusually expensive, so they didn't think they had to mention it. They each just bought a lot of little things, without telling each other. A month after the honeymoon they received their bill—and a big shock.

To avoid this problem, figure into your honeymoon budget an identical sum for each of you to spend as you wish. This money should be responsibility-free; if either of you chooses to use it to light cigars or to make airplanes with, fine. It should be "mad" money in the most complete sense, and criticizing how the other spends his or her mad money should be forbidden.

What if you find, to your dismay, that your budget is so small that almost every option is too expensive? Your choices then depend on how important the honeymoon is to you and how patient you both are. You could establish your honeymoon fund and delay the wedding until you can afford to have the honeymoon you want. You could go on a two-day honeymoon and save up for another honeymoon later on—a couple in love can't have too many! People are usually sympathetic to newlyweds, so if you ask your friends and relatives, perhaps they or someone they know could lend you a cabin or apartment for a few days. In this chapter (and here and there in others) we suggest still other ways of honeymooning on a very small budget. With ingenuity, the problem can be solved!

HONEYMOON BUDGET

CASH AVAILABLE:

Savings (per month)	$_____	
Total savings	_____	
Family	_____	
Other	_____	
TOTAL CASH AVAILABLE		$_____
Credit card post-honey-moon payments (per month)	$_____	
TOTAL HONEYMOON FUND		$_____

EXPENSES:

Major transportation

Basic rate		$_____
Additional fees:		
Excess luggage	$_____	
Luggage handling tips	_____	
Insurance	_____	
Airport taxes, similar levies	_____	
Gas	_____	
Other	_____	
TOTAL EXTRAS		$_____

Local transportation

To and from airports,
trains, etc. $_____

In-town/around resort area   _____

Side trips   _____

Other   _____

     TOTAL LOCAL $_____

Accommodations

Basic rate $_____

Additional fees:

     Meals $_____

     Sports/activities   _____

     Tips   _____

     Special services
     (flowers, etc.)   _____

     Other   _____

     TOTAL EXTRAS $_____

Entertainment

Sports $_____

Theater/concerts   _____

Museums   _____

Nightclubs/discos   _____

Sightseeing tours   _____

Other   _____

     TOTAL $_____

Gifts/souvenirs

Family $_____

Friends   _____

Us   _____

     TOTAL $_____

Mad money

Bride $_____

Bridegroom   _____

     TOTAL $_____

Emergency $_____

TOTAL EXPENSES $_____

Time is another important consideration. For instance, *when* you'll be able to go on your honeymoon affects *where* you'll be able to go. If you'd like to honeymoon at an American ski resort and you're getting married in August, there isn't much hope of that dream coming true. You'll have to go out of the country or choose something else. Also, if you'll be honeymooning at a place during its peak season, it will be more expensive for you.

The second time factor concerning your honeymoon is *how long* you have for the trip itself (including travel time), and *how long* it takes you to get where you're going. If your time is limited, you'll have to decide whether a faraway place is important enough to you to spend the time traveling, or whether you should find another place requiring less travel time.

The **two of you,** of course, are the most important factor to be considered, since a honeymoon that fails to be enjoyable and to enrich you would be pointless. Every place isn't going to please every person, so you have to know some important things about yourselves and keep these in mind. It's fun and revealing to sit down together and make lists of what you each enjoy, what you hate, and which activities you take part in regularly. Then compare your lists. Your honeymoon choice would, ideally, allow both of you to do things you enjoy and avoid things you dislike.

There are other qualities about both of you that aren't reducible to lists. For instance, are you shy? Outgoing? What are your values? Do you dislike fancy things and flashy people, or do you consider these things and people exciting? If you've never stayed in an expensive hotel before, do you think you would enjoy being fussed over by maids in your room, by three waiters and a wine steward in the dining room—or just be annoyed? No matter how beautiful or unique a place may be, if it isn't suited to you, the honeymoon could turn out to be, at best, disappointing.

In going over all the information you receive, check it against your inner knowledge about yourself and your mate-to-be.

In reading brochures ask yourself these questions:

· *What audience does it appeal to?* Couples, singles, families? Young, middle-aged, or older? Does the audience it's appealing to include *you?*

- *What does it concentrate on selling?* Accommodations, food, entertainment, location (seaside, rural, city), sports, total environment (as in a honeymoon lodge)? And how interested are you in what they're selling?
- *How does it describe the accommodations?* Are they deluxe, first-class, standard, tourist, superior? Does the seller define these standards in the same way as you do?
- *How far will you have to travel to get there?* Can you get there in a way that is both comfortable and convenient for you?
- *What other places of interest are located nearby?* Some resorts are located in isolated areas, so that you're almost forced to stay on their premises; others are near various interesting places. If a place is isolated, does it offer enough to make up for the lack of outside attractions?
- *Do they offer package plans?* These are easiest for you to use, and often less expensive than paying separately for the things included in the package. But will you take sufficient advantage of the activities offered to make the package price a true bargain? Try not to pay for features you won't be using.
- *What is the price range?* Even if it's a package price, you'll be spending money on tips and various kinds of "extras." Be wary of committing yourself to any honeymoon plan that comes very close to costing the maximum of what you can spend—you can too easily ruin your budget.
- *How large is the place?* Do you want to be part of a small group, or part of a larger group in which you have more chance of meeting new friends? Will a smaller place offer you all the services and activities you want? Would you prefer the more personalized service of a smaller place?
- *What meals are included?* American Plan (AP) means three meals a day are included in the price of accommodations; Modified American Plan (MAP) means two meals a day; European Plan (EP) means no meals included; and Continental Plan (CP) means rolls and coffee for breakfast are provided. On the MAP, can you choose which two meals? If meals are included, can you order à la carte without paying extra, or do you have to order from a specific menu?

- *What is the general style of the place*—dressy or casual?
- *What, if any, extras are offered to honeymooners?*

If you are going on a tour or if sightseeing is included in your package, be sure to ask:

- *What are the specifics?* How much time is allowed at specific stops? Are admission fees and tips included in the overall cost? What are the seating arrangements? Do you have the same guide throughout? What is the mode of transportation? Are there toilets? Air conditioning? No-smoking sections?
- *Are there hidden extras?* Does the length of your tour include the time spent in transit? Are airport taxes or other government-imposed levies included in the cost? Does the cost include tips to bellhops, waiters, chambermaids, local tour drivers and escorts?

Also, when reading brochures pay close attention to the pictures. Some cruise companies have brochures that show happy groups of senior citizens playing shuffleboard. If you're an older couple yourself, this might be just what you're looking for. If you're a much younger couple, it's not.

It's fun to learn about new places, especially when you might soon be visiting one of them! The more you learn, the better your chance of finding your perfect honeymoon spot, and you'll enjoy learning together.

You can use the following chart to compare some of the places you may be considering for your honeymoon.

Special Situations

Second and other honeymoons. Whether you've been married before, to someone else or to the person you are now remarrying, or whether you have lived together for some length of time, your honeymoon style is up to you. You can call it a vacation (knowing in your hearts that it's a honeymoon), or set off fireworks and announce the news to the world. It's all according to your temperaments and the customs of the place where you live.

GENERAL LOCATION COMPARISON CHART

PLACE _____

Cost for transportation _____	Climate	
Travel time necessary _____	Temperature range _____	
Transportation available	Humidity level _____	
Plane _____	Other _____	
Train _____	Locale	
Ship _____	Large city _____	
Bus _____	Small town _____	
Auto _____	Countryside _____	
Other _____	Mountains _____	
Accommodation price range	Seashore _____	
Hotel _____	Desert _____	
Motel _____	Plains _____	
Resort _____	Island _____	
Inn _____	Foreign _____	
Private home _____	Domestic _____	
Campground _____	Activities available	
	(fill in those desired)	

ACCOMMODATIONS COMPARISON CHART

PLACE _____

Basic cost _____	Steam room/sauna/	
Package rate _____	gym _____	
Type of accommodation	Auto parking _____	
Single room _____	General clientele	
Suite _____	Age range _____	
Cabin _____	Couples/families/	
Items included in price	mixed _____	
Meals	Facilities	
(how many) _____	Modern or older _____	
Sports/recreation	Number of units _____	
facilities _____	Resort or regular _____	
Local	Special courtesies for	
transportation _____	newlyweds (list)	
Tips for staff _____		

Special features of accommodations	
Large tubs/ mini-pools	———
Sauna	———
Radio/music	———
Television/ adult movies	———
Fireplace	———
Refrigerator/bar	———
Kitchenette	———
Mirrored walls/ ceilings	———
Extra-large beds	———
Vibrator beds	———
Satin sheets	———
Down pillows	———
Other	———
Availability of:	
Beauty parlor/ barber shop	———
Car rental	———
Child-care facilities	———
Cocktail lounge	———
Dancing Live/disco	———
Drugstore	———
Facilities for handicapped	———
Game room	———
Gift shop	———
Housekeeping services	———
Laundry/dry cleaning Same day or overnight	———
Live entertainment Type	———
Medical facilities	———
Movies	———
Photographer	———
Religious services	———
Room service Hours available	———
Shopping facilities	———
Sightseeing tours	———
Social director	———
Special diet	———
Sports pro	———
Sports/recreation (list)	

For couples who've lived together so long that everyone thinks they're already married, a honeymoon can be an opportunity to become legally wed. Simply take a honeymoon in your own state and have the marriage performed while you're away from home. No explanations, no fuss—in fact, a romantic elopement!

A honeymoon is a beginning, a time to renew your love, a symbol of commitment—it really has very little to do with the past.

Children? A honeymoon is a time for a couple to grow closer together, to devote time and love solely to one another. Although children can be delightful and can add many pleasures to any trip you might take with them, one of the things they won't enhance in any way is romance—a primary ingredient in a honeymoon!

What if a child wants to come along on the honeymoon? Gently but firmly explain that adults who get married need this time alone together, after which they'll return and enjoy taking care of their children. Even if a child protests or seems hurt by being excluded from your honeymoon, stand firm. It will be good for the child to realize that adults have needs and desires that must be respected.

What arrangements can be made for the care of your children while you're honeymooning? If you have willing and loving relatives, your problems are solved. For school-aged children, you might consider honeymooning in the summer and giving the child a choice of summer sleep-away camps to attend for a few weeks (many children would choose this before accompanying you on your honeymoon!).

You might find your regular baby-sitter willing to take care of your child if you'll be honeymooning for a short period of time, say two or three days. Finally, you may have a friend who would gladly care for your child during this period of time. If you can arrange child care for only a few days, do so, and then honeymoon in luxury and privacy.

What if you simply must take one or more children on your honeymoon? You might just have to shrug and accept the fact that your first honeymoon will be a family affair, but plan for a private honeymoon in the near future. If money is no problem, you could stay at a resort that offers a full children's program. Many cruise ships (mostly the larger ones) offer this same advantage. The children are kept happy and away from the adults through most of the day, and baby-sitting is available at night.

Just remember that it's only natural for a child to feel somewhat abandoned when you leave him or her to go on your honeymoon. Be firm, but reassuring and kind, and make plans for a short family vacation, if possible, in the near future.

Handicapped people. Since each person's handicap or illness is different, we can't begin to advise on particulars. Do, however, make sure that you begin planning your honeymoon well in advance—a minimum of six months ahead—and that you advise everyone concerned, in every letter, during every phone call, of your special requirements.

When you begin planning your honeymoon, you'll be pleased to find that restrictions which were operative even five years ago no longer exist, and that your honeymoon options are broader than you might have suspected. For detailed information on travel agents and groups that promote travel for the handicapped, call or write your state organization for persons with your difficulty, or write to: S.A.T.H. (Society for the Advancement of Travel for the Handicapped), 26 Court Street, Brooklyn, N.Y. 11242. Many other useful resources for the handicapped are listed in the back of this book.

Your animal friend. Basically, your pet doesn't belong on your honeymoon unless you're going polar-bear hunting at the North Pole and your dog is not only a husky, but a lead sled dog! Cats, birds, and fish are less likely to be even considered as honeymoon companions, so just think about dogs. Most hotels, motels, and resorts won't allow them. They are not allowed in many forests and on most beaches. If you take them into the wilderness, they're liable to pick up strange ticks and fleas and, if they have any initiative, to run off after wild game. This is not only likely to get them lost, but makes them legally vulnerable to being shot by hunters and game wardens protecting the wildlife.

Yes, your pet will miss you, but since animals lack a sense of time, one day of missing you is no more or less unpleasant than a week of missing you. Leave your pet with a willing friend or relative or board him or her with a vet.

3. THE ART OF TRAVEL

A TERRIFIC HONEYMOON requires more imagination and advance planning than money, and this is true whether you'll be honeymooning at a resort, a big-city hotel, a rustic campsite, or on a sailboat.

What makes a honeymoon great?

The right *location*—a place suited to your particular needs and desires.

Having things go smoothly because you've taken the time to come up with a practical *plan*.

The relaxed *attitude* you have when things are well thought out and under control.

Planning your honeymoon is an enjoyable opportunity for the two of you to learn and grow together. Take the dominant role in making arrangements, even if you're using the services of a travel agent.

The Importance of Planning

Nothing is more unromantic than rushing madly about, totally disorganized. Rushing is usually the result of poor planning. If you anticipate problems before they arise, you can either avoid them or be ready to deal with them.

For instance, let's suppose you've decided to go to one of the Caribbean islands for a week. You need to think ahead, about questions like these: What visas (if any) will you need? Will you need a passport? Vaccinations? What will the climate be like during the time you'll be there? Will you need a car? Do you need to learn some basic foreign phrases, or do the "natives" speak English? What items can you bring into the country and what can you bring back to the United States? Don't assume that everything will just somehow "work out"—many couples have their first marital argument over things that could have been avoided had they spent more time in planning.

Here are some basic keys to planning your honeymoon:

Give yourselves time. Two months is just about the minimum and six months isn't too long. You'll have plenty of time to look into all the options available, to investigate and find the perfect honeymoon spot. Planning this far ahead also allows you to make your reservations far in advance, so that you can take advantage of discounts. If your original plan turns out to be impractical or impossible, you'll still have time to make other arrangements.

Start a honeymoon fund as soon as you decide to get married. This should be a savings account separate from any others either of you may have; and it should require *both* your signatures for a withdrawal. It's hard to save money, but you can if you will sit down, figure out what each of you can contribute each week, and *stick to it.* It's better to promise a modest sum you know you can save, rather than a larger amount that might become a serious burden. Start this account even if you're expecting relatives to fund your honeymoon; if you don't need any or all of the money in the account, it will provide you with a financial cushion or perhaps go toward furnishing your new home. This is a good time for you to begin cooperating with each other and sharing in financial concerns.

Do research. Invest in a guidebook or two; read travel columns in bride's and other magazines; talk to people who've been to the places you're considering.

Start a honeymoon notebook. List things to see and places to shop or eat, along with such important information as their addresses, phone numbers, and the hours they open and close.

Making Arrangements

Hotels and motels. Make your reservations as far in advance as possible. Most major cities host hundreds of conventions a year, and good rooms are often at a premium. Ask the hotel to write back confirming your reservations, so you won't arrive to find there's "no room."

Follow up with a letter (keep a copy for yourself) specifying the arrangements and requesting a written confirmation. Allow plenty of time to receive a confirmation in writing. If time does not permit a written confirmation, be sure to get a confirmation number by telephone. Have this confirmation letter or number ready when you check in.

If you want a particular type of room or a special view, a bedroom-and-parlor suite, a kitchen, or whatever, spell it out in full in writing. If your hotel or motel is situated by a lake or the ocean, be sure to ask for a room that overlooks the water. Mention any special extras you'd like the hotel or resort to attend to—a bottle of champagne or basket of fruit on arrival, flowers delivered during your honeymoon, reservations for entertainment or sports activities, and so on. If you have a car, you'll want to inquire about garage arrangements.

Don't hide the fact that you'll be honeymooners. Hotels and resorts see honeymooners as the best kind of customers and often go out of their way to make your special stay with them unforgettable. So when you write or call for reservations, inform them that you'll be newlyweds. Your travel agent will do so if he or she makes the arrangements.

You might want to send a deposit for the first night of your stay and ask for a guaranteed reservation. The best way to guarantee a room is to charge your reservation to a credit card. This way you will have a record of the transaction. If you don't show up you still pay, but the hotel can't give away your room if you're late arriving. You can also specify a late arrival time—giving the hotel personnel some idea of when you'll be getting there. Most hotels won't hold unguaranteed reservations past a certain point, around dinnertime usually, unless you contact them.

One of the advantages of spending your wedding trip at a resort, particularly a honeymoon resort such as those in the Pocono Mountains of Pennsylvania, is that you won't have to worry about your accommodations being given away. You'll make a package arrangement with the resort for room and meals and it will all be covered by payment before you even arrive. With everything prepaid, you won't have to carry much money—just bring enough funds for any little extras you may want and tips for the resort staff upon leaving. Your resort will advise you of what's covered and what's extra in your prepaid arrangement. Here again, though, if you're delayed, inform the resort management.

Automobiles. If the hotels are busy you can be sure that the car rental companies will be busy too, and that there will be fewer cars available. Reserve your car as far in advance as possible and, again, ask for written confirmation, if there is enough time to get it.

If you're driving your own car, get details about overnight parking fees and find out if there's a charge for taking your car out of the garage in hotels that park cars without a fee. Also check about the local gasoline situation: will you be able to "fill 'er up" without difficulty?

If you're not driving your own car, find out if the hotel or resort you've selected is on the regular route of an airport bus or limousine, or if you can make advance arrangements to be picked up by the establishment's limousine—often at no charge. If it doesn't provide this service and is located some distance from the airport or bus or train depot, the expense of taking a taxi to get to your destination could range from irritating to stunning, and could put quite a dent in your "extras" budget. When you leave your resort or hotel, reserve space in its limousine the day before you leave.

Transportation. Transportation arrangements are covered thoroughly in the next chapter. Just remember that you can't make airplane ticket reservations too early. Buying your tickets several months ahead might result in tremendous savings for you.

Choosing and Using a Travel Agent

Who should use a travel agent? The inexperienced traveler, the busy traveler, anyone who can't keep informed on the latest travel bargains (which is almost all of us), the person who isn't good at, or just dislikes, details—*you,* if you want to leave the nitty-gritty arrangements to someone else so you can concentrate on all the activities that surround getting married.

Travel agents are paid a commission by the sellers of services —suppliers of transportation or accommodations—so there is normally no charge to you. Their basic functions are to help you choose between various options and to obtain bus, train, boat, or plane tickets, hotel accommodations, and package-tour reservations. They also can tell you about any seasonal events taking place in an area during your honeymoon and advise you about the climate and what type of clothing you'll need.

Many travel agents offer additional services. They can arrange for car rentals, sightseeing tours, and theater and sports tickets.

They can sell insurance to cover yourselves (a regular life insurance policy is a better investment than travel insurance) and your baggage (do get this, plus trip-cancellation insurance), help get passports and visas, and even advise you about where to shop.

Because they book in volume, agents often can get priority bookings or last-minute bookings that you couldn't get yourself. They keep on top of the latest bargains in travel. Since they're aware of conditions in any given place, they can keep you from going to the "wrong" place—where there's an outbreak of disease, political unrest, or where the crowd tends to be older or family-oriented (and hence probably not suited to honeymooners).

In almost every community, you're likely to find a travel agency within driving distance. In larger cities you can choose from travel agencies that specialize in planning tours for couples, tours in particular countries, or other "special" trips.

The best way to locate an agent is through word-of-mouth—

the recommendation of a satisfied traveler whose advice you trust. Ask if the agent is a member of the American Society of Travel Agents. When you visit an agency look for a neat, clean, organized office, amply furnished with brochures. An organized office probably indicates that the agents will be organized about arranging your wedding journey.

You should go into an agency with a good idea of approximately *how much money* you can spend, *when* you're going to be taking your honeymoon, and either the *kind of place* or the *activity* that is most important to you. The agent should allow you to talk about yourselves for a reasonable amount of time so that he or she will have an idea of what you're like and what kind of place would suit you. Some places are not good for young, inexperienced travelers, and your agent will probably point these out to you. Leave these for later trips.

Since they make their money from commissions, some agents are prone to direct you into the higher-priced package tours that are the least work for them. If you're very sure that you want your own, individual tour and the agent won't cooperate, you'll have to look for another agent. You can also plan and make arrangements for all or some of the trip yourselves. For instance, you might use your agent to make passport, visa, plane, and first-night hotel arrangements, and then make the reservations yourselves for the other places you want to visit.

After this first visit to the travel agent, you'll probably come home with brochures—study them. Even if you had something else in mind, you might find out about a tour or a place that seems better than your original idea. Once you know what interests you, use your agent to chase down details and give you an estimate of total costs. Your agent should also help you compare services and accommodations in relation to costs. Once your plans are firm and your agent is ready to make the arrangements, ask how soon you'll get confirmations on your transportation and accommodations. Be sure that you get vouchers for all hotels or other accommodations. If your original plan falls through, you'll need to know as soon as possible, so you can make new arrangements.

As soon as an agent accepts you as a client, he or she should explain all charges. If you're simply taking a package tour that includes air fare, transportation to the resort, a week's stay, and all meals, there should be no fee to you. If, however, the agent has to make toll phone calls, write extra letters, or change your reservations after they've been made, you'll be charged a fee. Some agents will charge you for every change you make after okaying a trip plan.

If you have a problem during your trip, report complaints to your agent as soon as you get home. He or she may be able to get you a partial refund and will discourage other clients from using the same facilities if the situation isn't corrected. If you have a problem with a travel agent, you should contact the American Society of Travel Agents and Better Business Bureau. You also can go to Small Claims Court, in which case you should take along your notes of all meetings or discussions with the agent regarding your trip arrangements—plus correspondence from the agent with specifics of your arrangements. It's always a good idea to ask for written confirmation from agents, hotels, airlines, and others involved in your honeymoon trip.

How to Save Money on Your Honeymoon— Without Scrimping!

Herewith some short and pertinent suggestions that will cut the cost of your honeymoon without decreasing your enjoyment— and, in some cases, will actually *increase* it.

- Stay longer in fewer places—not only is going from one place to another tiring—it's *expensive!* Far better for you as honeymooners to take the time to choose a good location and stay there. If you choose one location and explore it well, you'll really get to know the people and place, rather than having a sort of three-dimensional postcard knowledge of what the place is about. You'll also save on transportation, tips, and sight-seeing.
- Stay in a budget motel if the area you're seeing is the at-

traction—you might be able to save enough to add an extra day or two to your honeymoon.

- Conversely, cut your honeymoon short by a day or two in order to enjoy better accommodations, if that's important to you. This can mean freedom from money worries and might be more worthwhile to you than a longer, more budget-conscious honeymoon would be.

- Choose a popular spot at an unpopular time of the year. Most places have to keep their help and keep their facilities up even during "off" seasons. Many ski resorts, for instance, offer lovely spring, summer, and fall accommodations for a fraction of the winter price. Look into these.

- Travel the cheapest possible way to save money for your honeymoon destination. If you know you'll have more money once you arrive, the no-frills travel will be easy to tolerate.

- Plan well ahead and make your reservations early. You may realize a big saving.

- Travel off-hours and midweek, if possible, and be flexible. If inflation or a tight budget has priced your first choice out of range, have a second or third option in mind and be ready to take advantage of that.

- Travel family plan, if possible. By the time you leave for your honeymoon you'll be a family—so take advantage of these discounts.

- Avoid excess baggage charges. If you're flying to your honeymoon, find out what you can take without extra charge. Consult one another and try to stay below the limit. Not only will this save you money, it'll help you avoid dragging along more baggage than you need—and leave room for the additions you pick up during your travels.

- If you're booking yourselves, shop around for the cheapest fare.

- Use a travel agent—if you're happy with one of the tours available, you'll save a significant amount of money.

- Don't automatically choose to fly. There are bus or train deals that not only will save you money, but will provide you with an interesting, if longer, journey to your honeymoon destination.

- Choose a hotel room where you have cooking facilities. These *are* more expensive, but if one or both of you likes to cook, you'll save money by not eating out and tipping.
- Dine at noon—have a big lunch, rather than a heavy dinner. Restaurant prices are higher in the evening.
- Picnic—you'll not only "get back to nature" and enjoy a wonderfully fun and romantic meal, but save money by buying bread, cheese, fruit, and wine and taking off for the countryside.
- If you're going abroad, go "native . . ." Stay where the locals stay, eat where they eat, shop where they shop. You'll save money and get to know the country and its people much better than the average tourist. Just remember that the level of accommodations may not be up to those of most American hotels. You might not have a private bathroom, for instance.
- American cigarettes and liquor are expensive in foreign countries. You can, however, buy the legal limit at the duty-free airport shop before takeoff. Your purchases will be delivered to you on your plane.
- The European bus and subway systems are efficient and economical means of transportation. If you plan to tour by taxicab, it may be less expensive to hire a driver for the day.

The Artful Traveler

The artful traveler expects to meet friendly, cooperative people—and does; is interested in other people's ways of doing things; and takes minor inconvenience with a shrug. The artful traveler is open and eager to learn. If you've never traveled before—or never traveled extensively—and all this seems complicated to you, take heart: even the travel experts and advisers were beginners once. Don't be afraid to reveal your lack of experience. Ask questions. Asking questions and trying new things is how everyone learns. Learn together—and enjoy!

4. PRACTICAL TIPS
ABOUT GETTING THERE

Planning Your Itinerary

AN ITINERARY is a record of a trip, in this case, a *pre*-record of your honeymoon that'll allow you to move smoothly from one place and activity to another. Your three most valuable aids in planning your itinerary are a *telephone,* a *calendar,* and a *notebook.*

A *telephone* is invaluable for checking with your travel agent, getting information, and making any reservations you'll be handling personally. Don't rely, however, on the telephone solely. Once you've made a firm commitment—to a particular plan your travel agent suggests, to take a flight, to stay at a resort—follow up immediately with a letter that spells out exactly what the arrangement is to be. Ask that the other persons involved respond to your written confirmation. This is the best way to avoid misunderstandings.

Your *calendar* comes into use as you begin making concrete arrangements and as dates fall into place. Record appointments with your travel agent and for vaccinations, times and places of departures, check-ins, and so on. When you go on your honeymoon take the calendar with you and use it to record activities you wish to participate in. This becomes another memento of your honeymoon.

Buy a *notebook* as soon as you know you'll be honeymooning and use the first section to list possible honeymoon spots (save the first two sheets for this). Use the second section as a planner, recording things that have to be done. A typical entry might read something like this:

May 15 (Tuesday)

WENDY: Pick up brochures on Mexico, Caribbean, Puerto Rico before Friday night.

STU: Go to library, get books on scuba diving, apply for credit card.

As your plans become settled, write them down in this section and review it now and again. This will help keep you in control of the trip.

Use the third section for a honeymoon diary, and any other sections for autographs, poems, and whatever else you'd like to remember.

Getting from Here to There

Your method of transportation—or combinations—will depend on several factors. Usually, the choice will almost make itself, as some options turn out to be the easiest or most convenient. But there are also factors that relate to your own expectations for this important trip.

Do you have a choice? Sometimes it's this easy—wonderful Mount Crisko, favorite of hot-dog skiiers all over the world, can only be reached by car or train. You don't have a car or don't drive. Hello train.

Do you hate traveling? If you do, you'll naturally choose the fastest possible way to get where you're going.

Do you love traveling? If you can answer this with a resounding "yes," then you may want to take a slower method of transportation—train or ship, for instance, instead of a plane.

How much time do you have? No matter how much you love traveling, if you have a three-day honeymoon you'll want to get there as fast as you can.

Do you have more time than money? If this is your situation, then you can shop around for the least expensive transportation you can get, even if it's slow.

You can probably think of other circumstances, based on your personal situation, that will influence your choice. Your health, eligibility for discounts (if one of you works for an airline, for instance), emotional preferences, and luck will all play a part in helping you choose. But the most important factor is *planning*. Gather information. Think about it. Choose. Make arrangements. Go!

Here is a brief and general discussion of various modes of transportation. It should give you some background on what the *experience* of traveling via car, plane, train, ship, or bus is like. When you begin planning your honeymoon itinerary you should investigate the services available in your particular area.

Automobiles

Your automobile gives you the most individual freedom of any form of transportation. Wherever there's a public road—concrete, tar, or dirt—there you can go, according to your whim and sense of adventure. Your car can get you to out-of-the-way places that would take several transfers to reach via public transportation. Some areas are very inconvenient if you don't have a car—places where public transportation is spotty or nonexistent. Furthermore, a car gives you the option of stopping at interesting sights, whether antique stores, gambling casinos, or pretty streams; of changing your destination on the spur of the moment; of exploring tree-shadowed country roads.

If you'll be driving to your honeymoon destination, follow these suggestions to ensure that your trip will be safe and relaxing.

Before you leave:
· Plan your trip with maps, figuring out your route and how long it will take you to reach various points in your journey. Leave a copy of this itinerary (a schedule of *where* you'll be *when*) with a responsible friend or relative.
· Leave duplicates of your car and house keys with someone.
· Make sure you have specific travel directions to your destination, that the directions are clear, and that you understand them.
· Have your car checked at the garage. Check the water level

in the battery, the level of windshield-washer fluid, and the tires, which should not be over- or under-inflated. Make sure your spare tire is inflated and usable. Have a tune-up and oil change. Get your car lubricated.

- Be sure to take your driver's licenses, car registration, and insurance card.
- Have a medical emergency kit, flares, and distress flag in the car.
- If it's winter, try to carry two thermal blankets (available at sporting-goods stores) or four wool ones in the car.

On the road:

- Do *not* exceed the speed limit, no matter how much behind schedule you are. The possible consequences of speeding give the old saying "better late than never" a grim meaning.
- Don't ever drink before driving or while driving—the latter is a felony.
- Use your seat belts
- Try to do all your driving in the daytime. If that isn't possible, stop every two hours at night and walk around for five or ten minutes.

Saving gasoline: With the high cost of gasoline these days, being economical with your fuel is more than common sense—it's necessary. The key is *moderation*. Accelerate gradually; drive at a steady speed; don't push the accelerator down all the way when driving up a long hill; pace yourself. If you see you're approaching a red light or stop sign, slow down gradually—don't speed up to the stop and then slam on the brakes.

Use a good gasoline, have periodic tune-ups, and make sure your tires are inflated to the right pressure. Eliminate any extra weight of unnecessary attachments, such as tire chains and ski racks in the summer. Operate the air conditioner only when you need it. If you have a choice of rental cars, take the one that gets the most mileage to the gallon. When possible, travel during off-peak hours. Try to use routes that have a minimum of traffic lights and stop signs.

Auto Clubs: A full-service auto club can save you money and makes things easier for you at a very modest annual fee—probably less than it would cost you to get towed one time. Most auto clubs offer the following benefits to their members:

- *Emergency road service*—Towing, fixing a flat, delivering gasoline, jumping a dead battery, and minor repairs are all paid for by the auto club. You pay for any parts and, of course, for gasoline.
- *Planning a trip*—All auto clubs will help you plan a car trip. They'll also give you an information packet containing things like travel tips, a full map of the U.S., and a map of your route.
- *Emergency travel expenses*—A full-service club will reimburse you for transportation and other expenses that might result from your having an accident with your car (there's a limit to how much they'll pay).
- *Travel insurance*—An integral part of membership in any of the full-service clubs, this insurance is limited to travel-related accidents.
- *Other services*—In addition to the services already mentioned, auto clubs pay a reward for information leading to the arrest and conviction of anyone who steals a member's car, will help you with bail if you're arrested for a traffic violation (except for felony offenses or drunken driving), and will help pay legal fees if you have to appear in court.

Renting a car: If you'd like to drive to your honeymoon place but don't have a car, or don't want to use yours, use somebody else's. Renting a car for special occasions can be a lot less expensive than owning one. You save the costs of insurance and maintenance, and if anything goes wrong, the car is either repaired at the company's expense or replaced. You might also choose to rent a car to save wear and tear on your own, or to have the use of a smaller or larger car than the one you own.

Generally, anyone with a valid driver's license and acceptable credit identification can rent a car. Few companies rent to anyone under twenty-one; some won't rent to anyone under twenty-five. A credit card is almost indispensable. Thefts have made car-rental firms nervous, so your innocent face (even if combined with lots of cash) won't make any difference. You might be able to get around this by going to a smaller rental agency along with a friend or relative. You quite properly sign up as the driver, with the card-holding friend or relative putting his or her credit on the line. Big companies won't do this, but some smaller ones will. It's worth a try.

Rental agencies offer many different types of cars and various time/mileage/price deals. Investigate several companies and keep asking until you find the right package to suit your needs. *Rates vary widely.* In deciding what plan is best for you, work out your planned mileage per day and be sure not to underestimate. If your original plans for use of a rented car change, your quoted charges may change too. Most agencies have preferred rates based on length of time and days of the week on which the car is rented; costs vary depending on where the car is returned.

Don't rent from a company that stalls or refuses to provide insurance information, or that rents cars without proper insurance coverage. And when the rental agent asks if you want all types of insurance—standard liability, personal accident or injury, comprehensive (theft, vandalism), and collision coverage—you may want to take the complete package. The cost is probably low and a good value. Some companies include a complete insurance package without charge—ask about this.

Before leaving the rental agency, check the car carefully. Check the directional signals, brakes, windshield wipers, and horn. Make sure there is a decent spare tire and a jack in the trunk. When you're out on the road, it's too late to make an exchange or correct the situation.

If you'll be driving through Europe, keep these three things in mind:

1. You'll need a Green Card—an international certificate attesting that you have adequate insurance coverage on your car. For crossing most European borders this is more important than your passport.
2. In many (but not all) countries you'll need an international driver's license. Get this in the U.S. before leaving.
3. Gas prices are very high and differ a lot over national borders —you could save money by filling up in a less expensive

country before crossing the border or, if you're staying near a border, simply crossing over to fill up.

Airplanes

What is it about flying that's so romantic? Is it the deep hum of the engines, the buoyant sensation of being borne on the wind? City, town, field, and forest dwindle, becoming patterns. Up high, the sky is huge. The sun or moon shines down on the carpeting clouds. Meanwhile, inside the plane, people talk and read, watch movies, and eat. They act as though this extraordinary thing—riding through the air at hundreds of miles an hour—were perfectly ordinary.

If you choose, you can fly first class and dine elegantly miles high above the earth. For long flights, some airlines now offer sleeping accommodations or small private rooms with seats that convert to beds. But even on the most inexpensive flight, you can enjoy the experience of flying and get to your destination quickly and safely.

Classes of air service: First class is by far the highest priced, but also the most luxurious. The seats are more comfortable, the meals better, and movies and drinks are free. Coach, sometimes called second class or tourist, is the least expensive. The coach section of the plane is usually more crowded, so that meal service can be slow. Standard means that all seats on the airplane are priced the same—there are no first-class seats or services.

Regularly discounted fares: Many flights can save you money. For instance, on domestic flights, if you stay over Saturday night in your farthest destination city, you'll always pay less. Savings can also be realized by flying on selected flights between 10 P.M. and 4 A.M., or on "no-frills" flights, which mean just that and more—you probably won't get food or drinks. (You *could* bring a picnic, though.)

Excursion fares are known by different names at different airlines. You have to buy these tickets well in advance and stay at your destination for a specified length of time, usually a week or more. Passengers flying together on a group plan don't necessarily know one another. They've signed up with various travel agents who sell group plans.

Making reservations is easy, thanks to the telephone. Just call any airline and ask if it flies to your destination. If it doesn't, it'll refer you to an airline that does, and sometimes even book the flight on that other airline for you. It'll also refer you to another company if it doesn't have a flight that leaves when you want to go.

Once you've found an airline that can service you, find out about the kind of seats available (first class or coach), ask when you should pick up and pay for your tickets (or request that they be mailed to you), and ask for the flight number and the flight departure and arrival times. This is also the time to request a particular seat—by the window or at the bulkhead—or any special meal (kosher, vegetarian, or salt-free, for instance), and to find out what your baggage allowance is.

The airline will confirm your reservations, either by calling you, or at the time when you call to make the arrangements. You should reconfirm by calling them twenty-four hours before a domestic flight and seventy-two hours before an international flight.

Buying your tickets: When you call to make your reservation, you'll be asked when you will pick up your tickets. You don't have to go to the ticket office or airport if you prepay by mail and have the tickets mailed to you. If you're expected to pick them up, however, and you won't be able to do so at or before the agreed time, advise the airline ticket office or travel agent. Otherwise, your reservations are likely to be cancelled.

Baggage: The airlines will give you free baggage identification labels at the ticket office or airport. You write your name and destination on the tag and tie or stick one on each bag. It's also a good idea to have your name, destination, and home address on the inside of your bags, in case the outer tag is lost. If you have old tags on your luggage, remove them. You don't want the baggage handlers to make a mistake and send your luggage to last year's vacation spot.

Get to the airport no later than thirty minutes before the flight so that your luggage can be loaded. An hour is better, since check-in and security clearance can be slow during peak flying periods. Keep your carry-on luggage to a minimum. Carry all valuables—jewelry, traveler's checks, cash, or business papers—on your person or with you.

Ships

In "Planning Your Honeymoon" we considered the romance of a seagoing honeymoon. Here we'll discuss taking a voyage to your honeymoon destination—a great way to unwind while "getting there." Because our everyday lives are run by the clock, the notion of the "timeless time" of shipboard life, with only pleasant activities and bells announcing meals to punctuate the day, can be appealing. You can swim in the pool and take nightly walks about the deck, watching the moon make silver patterns on the waves. Getting to your honeymoon location slowly allows you to relax after the wedding. By the time you get where you're going, you'll be fully into the relaxed and romantic mood that'll help you get the most enjoyment from your wedding trip and your first days together as husband and wife.

Who should use a ship as transportation? The couple who aren't on a tight schedule and are on their way to a seaside honeymoon. It isn't suitable for people who are short on time or who have a very small budget.

While you'll see cruises advertised in newspapers and magazines, these are usually for people who intend spending all their trip on the ship, with a few short visits to interesting spots. To check on ships as a means of transportation, use the services of your travel agent. There are packages that combine a cruise to a resort, a few days or a week at the resort, and a flight home. A competent travel agent will know about these and will also be able to steer you clear of ships that attract primarily older people or families. You can also call or write the ticket office of several steamship companies and make inquiries just as you would with an airline.

Trains

Trains were once the preferred method of travel in the U.S., as they still are within Europe. They dwindled and now have staged something of a comeback, which well they should. Although they are not, of course, as fast as planes, you can get to many of the same places for less money on a train and without worrying about bad weather if you're a nervous flier. Unlike airports, train stations are generally located in town, which makes it easier for you to get around once you reach your destination. Traveling by train doesn't tire you as much as driving would.

American rail lines—having once again begun to court the public—have come up with several innovations of interest to honeymooners. Some offer transparent-roofed sightseeing cars, dining or snack cars, and, on some runs, live entertainment. On some trains you can get a small room for two with washstand and toilet and lounge seats that fold out into beds. During their declining years, after World War II, train companies lost their reputation for the elegant travel that had once featured dining cars rivaling fine restaurants and private cars that were rolling mansions. Modern trains may not match the splendor of their predecessors, but they have undergone improvement in food service and cleanliness.

Here is another opportunity for you to take advantage of your new family status. Amtrak, for instance, has a family ticket plan good for unlimited travel on certain days. Whichever rail service you choose, ask about special fare levels and restrictions.

Europe is famous for its train services, which take you all over the continent, through country and city, and across national borders. Experienced travelers recommend trains of the Trans-Europe-Express (TEE) and other "name" trains. The TEE trains are usually extra-deluxe and the food delicious. A Eurailpass (which can be purchased in advance only *before* leaving the U.S., *not* in Europe) gives you unlimited travel on most of these trains. In Britain, there's the Britrail pass for unlimited travel in the British Isles.

Here again you can use the suggestions given in the airline

section of this chapter: to get your tickets, call the rail lines that go where you want to go. They will help route you (if you need to switch trains), make reservations, and mail your tickets to you if you've paid in advance.

Traveling by train to your honeymoon is an adventure in itself. You see the countryside (good and bad), meet fellow travelers, and can still have the privacy you'll want, if you use a Slumbercoach compartment.

Bus

Who should take a bus? You should if that is the only way to reach your destination, as it sometimes is; if you'd rather not drive; if it's less expensive than a rent-a-car and your budget is small. Almost all buses in the U.S. are motor coaches, which have well-padded reclining seats, and toilets. Rather than tiring yourself by driving and looking for turns, you could relax and talk, play magnetic board games or word games, read, or just watch the countryside float by.

Some bus companies offer excursions (we talked about those in "Planning Your Honeymoon") with guides, but for getting-to-your-destination bus travel, you'll have to plan the trip yourself. Ordinarily, you would call the bus company that goes where you want to go, ask about departure times, and buy your ticket a half hour to an hour before the bus leaves. There is usually no reservation needed or available for this kind of trip. One final advantage of bus travel is that you can bring along as much luggage as you can carry for no extra charge.

The Travel Experience

As eager as you are to get to your honeymoon location, don't forget that "getting there" *is* half the trip. Be alert to what's going on around you and, if you can, take time to savor the experiences you'll be having. The pleasure you get from traveling is in direct proportion to the enthusiasm and good nature with which you approach it.

The following chart will help you decide which mode of transportation is right for you, based on the factors we've discussed in this chapter.

TRANSPORTATION COMPARISON CHART

TYPE/CARRIER _____

Cost
   Full fare
     (first class)   _____
   Full fare (coach)   _____
   Special rates   _____
   Package rates   _____

Terms
   Cancellation
     policy   _____
   Reservation
     deadline   _____
   Payment deadline   _____

Package includes
   (list items)

Time to reach
   destination   _____

Local transportation
   needed   _____
   Cost   _____

Number of transfers   _____
   Waiting time
     between   _____

Reconfirm prior to
   departure   _____
   How long before?   _____

Luggage handling
   Amount allowed   _____
   Extra fees   _____
   Tips   _____

Comfort of carrier
   (list features)

Facilities for
   handicapped   _____
Meals available   _____
   Extra costs   _____

Entertainment
   available
   Extra costs   _____

Sleeping
   accommodations   _____
   Extra costs   _____

Auto/camper rental
   Basic fee   _____
   Free mileage
     allowance   _____
   Insurance (per day):
     Collision   _____
     Liability   _____
   Rate for extra
     days   _____
   Gas: $_____ per gallon
     _____ mpg
   Estimated mileage _____

   TOTAL COST $_____

Section Two

PREPARING FOR THE JOURNEY

5. A TRUE APHRODISIAC: GOOD HEALTH

ALFRED KINSEY, the famous sex researcher, discovered only one true aphrodisiac in all his years of investigating: good health. His prescription for a satisfying love life, then, would have included a happy outlook, sensible diet, exercise, and outdoor activities—the same elements that lead to a happy life in general.

If you're in less than tip-top shape right now, why not make a health pact with your betrothed? Perhaps you both want to lose just a few pounds or get in better shape before the wedding. Do it *together*. Start right now to support each other and encourage each other to get and stay fit. Not only will you enjoy your activities together, but you'll spend more time together and work toward helping each other to be the very best you can be.

Here are some things you can do together now—before your honeymoon—that will bring you closer and help both of you to enhance your sex appeal.

Body Beautiful!

Dieting can be a drag if you're doing it alone, but if you both need to lose a little weight, do it together. You might be surprised at how much fun it can be! You can get together every evening and alternate cooking delicious low-calorie meals, cheering each other on as the weight begins to go down.

How long you have before your wedding determines how much weight you should try to lose. Most doctors (and, of course, you should see yours about a diet plan) now suggest trying for a weight loss of no more than a pound and a half to two pounds a week. This means the weight comes off very slowly, and the slowness is the advantage—by the time you've lost even five to ten pounds, you'll have changed your eating habits to some extent.

When you and your future husband or wife "gang up" on even a slight weight problem, you're going to win. Remember to keep your expectations realistic—that one or two pounds a week—and to bring as much fun to your weight-loss project as you can. Try preparing recipes from some of the low-calorie gourmet or ethnic cookbooks, and provide a romantic atmosphere for dining—flowers on the table, candlelight, music, the works!

Encourage each other and reward yourselves for your virtue with nonedible goodies—an extra hour in bed on a weekend, a sweater you've wanted, or a new record album. It's important, by the way, to tell yourself exactly what each reward is for. "I'm buying myself this record because I was great with the diet this week and didn't slip up even once!"

In Chapter 17 of this book, you will find more specific useful tips for making a diet successful.

Exercise

You can enjoy companionship even more when you team up for exercise and sports. Praise is a powerful thing! With each of you cheering the other on, you'll make faster progress and have more fun. If you're really in poor condition, you might want to try a gentle exercise plan at first: walking a mile a day, taking up yoga, or riding your bike. Do these things *together*. Make good health both a habit and a daily pleasure—not something you do to lose five pounds and then drop until the next time, when you have to lose ten.

Over a period of time, you can try different exercise systems. Not only will you find which ones work best for you, but trying new things will keep up your interest. Basically, you should try to engage in some form of vigorous exercise (jogging, swimming, racquetball) for a minimum of a half hour, three or four times a week. Calisthenics for toning can be done daily for fifteen minutes. And you might be interested to know that not only is exercise good for sex, but sexual activity is also a form of exercise!

Once you begin your honeymoon, you'll probably want to try some new activities. If you've already begun to shape up before your wedding trip, you'll be ready. Even so, be a little cautious. A sprained ankle or wrist is wretchedly painful, so don't try to be *too* heroic on the tennis court or with the volleyball team. And, of course, enjoy as many activities as you can *together*.

An Exercise Program

Exercise comes in many forms. You can choose from among calisthenics, skating, swimming (one of the best forms of overall exercise), skiing, tennis, jogging or running, dancing (ballet, belly, or disco are among your choices here), or any one of a number of other sports.

Regardless of the form of exercise you select, it is recommended that you begin with warm-up exercises and conclude with a cooling-down period. One suggested regime is:

- 7–8 minutes of warm-up—stretching, turning, twisting, and generally loosening up;
- 8–10 minutes of push-ups, sit-ups, pull-ups to strengthen arms, shoulders, thighs, and so forth;
- 30 minutes of activity at a pace brisk enough to elevate breathing and heart rate. You might select jogging, fast walking, running, jumping rope, bicycling;
- 5–7 minutes of cool-down, moving around slowly, and staying loose.

It's also recommended that you don't engage in strenuous sports on a full stomach and that you stop if you develop any tenderness.

THE PROS OF EXERCISE

1. Firms muscles; converts fat into muscle.
2. Dress in clothing that is light both in weight and color.

3. Increases stamina, coordination.
4. Reduces tension and fatigue.
5. Acts as a cardiovascular stimulus to strengthen your heart.

Safety First

HOT-WEATHER SAFETY TIPS

1. Take it easy.
2. Dress in clothing that is light both in weight and color.
3. Eat less, but be sure you're eating a balanced diet.
4. Drink lots of liquids to make up for the fluid you lose through perspiration. This should be a minimum of six to eight glasses of water a day.
5. Play active sports in the morning or evening when the temperature's apt to be lowest.
6. Just because the day is overcast does not mean you're protected from the dangers of heat and humidity.
7. Don't get too much sun. Get a suntan by gradual exposure.
8. Rest for ten minutes after every hour of activity. If you find the heat's getting to you, find a cool spot to relax in.
9. If you experience cramps, extreme fatigue, headache, dizziness, nausea, or vomiting, which are all symptoms of a hot-weather emergency, seek medical aid.

Stress

There are also some not-so-obvious health hazards you might run into on your honeymoon. Stress is one of them. As the wedding draws near and the honeymoon begins, the most loving person may become irritable, tense, and very tired—at the time when he or she expects to feel most happy and energetic! Worse, the "cold feet" that may have preceded the wedding can change into a panicky conviction that the whole marriage is a mistake.

Stress is related to happy events, just as to unhappy ones. It seems that *any* major event, good or bad, is stressful and can cause you to feel unbalanced physically and emotionally. It can creep up on you almost without your awareness, especially if you're very busy making arrangements and socializing. The first sign might be a skin problem, headaches, or sleeping difficulties, or maybe just irritableness.

As with virtually everything else from now on, talk to your future mate about this. He or she, after all, may be feeling some of the same things. During your honeymoon itself, if you find yourselves suffering from stress, you can avoid certain situations that will add to your discomfort—such as overcrowding or too much rushing around. Make sure that you have some time alone each day to relax.

Good Night

Sleep problems are related to stress. You may have trouble getting to sleep, staying asleep, or getting up on time. Sleep researchers have found that even missing an entire night or two of sleep has no serious effects—as long as it's only a night or two. So a night spent relaxing in bed, talking, and making love, even if followed by only an hour or two of sleep, could be a lovely experience, and won't do you any harm.

If you do have real, persistent problems getting to sleep or staying asleep, and this is related to the honeymoon stress we talked about before, the problem will gradually disappear as you settle into your new life. In the meantime, most sleep experts recommend that if you're incapable of sleeping after being in bed an hour or so, you should get up. A hot bath, reading, watching TV, or having a glass of milk (preferably warm) can help you relax enough to become drowsy. The experts also advise that you not worry about lack of sleep—it'll keep you awake.

Another sleep problem that might arise because of stress is snoring. Snores have been known to drive the most loving spouse from the marital bed and, in severe cases, all the way into another room at night. The U.S. Patent Office has approximately

four hundred antisnore devices filed—most of them worthy of
the Spanish Inquisition. Doctors, rushing to the rescue, have
come up with . . . nothing. Some people snore only when they're
very tired or under stress, so the problem is likely to clear up
pretty much by itself if it's related to either of these circumstances. If the non-snorer is really being kept awake by the
snoring, he or she could wear earplugs—it's better than giving
up a loving mate.

Perhaps you're wondering why we're discussing health in a
book on honeymooning. Next time you walk down the street,
look carefully at the people passing by. No matter what their
age, there are some people who are beautiful to look at, whether
they match up to ideal concepts of beauty or not. If you look
closer, you'll see all the signs of health: good muscle tone, clear
skin, bright eyes, and a graceful, energetic walk.

We hope that you and your mate look like this now, and in
ten years, and in forty years. This book is specifically about
honeymoons, but on a deeper level it's about beginning a life
together that is fulfilling and joyful. And we really don't think
you can have all the happiness you deserve from life unless
you're as healthy as it is possible for you to be.

6. TROUSSEAU:

HIS AND HERS

WHAT's special about the clothes you buy for your honeymoon?
In the most practical aspects, nothing. You choose additions to
your wardrobe that are suitable for your honeymoon spot, but
this is no different from buying clothes for an ordinary vacation.
If there's any difference at all, it's in how you feel about these

clothes. Being married is one of the most important things that will ever happen to you. Somehow it seems more important to look especially attractive for these first days and weeks as a married person. In addition, you'll feel more relaxed and comfortable if you're sure you look good.

This, then, is a natural time to take an honest look at yourself in a full-length mirror. Are you still clinging to styles that were popular five years ago? Do you dress in styles that looked good on you when you were a teenager, but that are now inappropriate? Perhaps you've gained or lost a significant amount of weight and need to take that into consideration.

No one—woman or man—should be so concerned with how he or she looks that it becomes a source of anxiety or discomfort. But caring about how you look in a moderate way is healthy. Someone who's sloppy and out-of-date in dress seems to be saying, "I'm not important enough to myself to take care of how I look." Do you want to say this to your mate? To your boss? To the world?

Finding your style means discovering what clothes look good on you and fit into the kind of life you lead in the place you live. It might help clarify your thinking if you sit down and write out the answers to the following questions:

- How do you spend most of your time? (Working in an office? At home? Doing physical work? In school?)
- What kinds of recreation do you take part in frequently? (Sports? Reading? Involvement in an organization?)
- What clothes that you already own do you find most comfortable—the ones you could just about live in?
- What do you want in the future from your career? Do you want to move into management or work toward a promotion? If so, you might want to start looking the part now.

The answers to these questions should give you a certain picture of yourself and your clothing needs. They should tell you what you need to replace (a new sweat shirt) or acquire (a more businesslike wardrobe if you're career-oriented; more casual clothes if you spend a lot of time participating in sports, for instance). Also, if the number of items on your "comfort" list are extremely few, you might need to choose clothing more carefully.

It's very heartening that styles have become more and more varied in the last decade or so. This means that you can find a look that suits and expresses *you,* rather than trying to conform to somebody else's "ideal." Because of this, we can't tell you what to wear or how to dress—nor would we want to. If you need help with finding your style, read men's or women's fashion magazines, and observe people who are close to you in age and physical characteristics and who look good. Try to figure out what they're doing right—it may work for you, too.

If you're relying mainly on fashion magazines, remember that they often show fashions at their most extreme. You'll need to adapt any styles you see there to your own life-style, individual looks, and locality. What looks stylish and sophisticated in New York City or Los Angeles might look eccentric and strange in Miller's Corner, Wyoming—and vice versa.

For instance, if jeans are your favorite garment, there's no need to give them up. But buy a good pair—tailored and proportioned to fit *you*—and wear them with a chic blouse or shirt and a sports jacket. Finish the whole thing off with good leather boots or sandals or clogs and some jewelry or a scarf. Without making any huge investments or making yourself uncomfortable, you'll have a stylish look.

Treat yourself to a really good haircut and have a manicure. Whether you're a man or woman, these two improvements in your appearance will quickly make a change for the better—again, without a large investment. Make sure that any clothing you own or buy fits well—or have it altered. Stick to good fabrics and avoid clothing with a lot of trim, which tends to look fussy.

No matter what your physical type—short and slim to tall and heavy, and every possible variation in between—you can look stylish and attractive. When you feel confident about your appearance, you come across as someone people want to know. It takes thought and planning to create an attractive and practical trousseau, but you'll still be enjoying your new look long after the honeymoon is officially over.

Begin planning your trousseau by finding out as much as possible about your honeymoon location. Your travel agent or someone at the hotel or resort where you'll be staying should be able to tell you what kinds of clothing are appropriate. Some resorts, for instance, are very casual and sporty during the day but dressy at night. Most big city hotels are fairly dressy day and night. Also, check out the differences in day and night temperatures. Sometimes, places that are hot during the day are cold at night. In addition, follow these suggestions to make choosing and wearing your honeymoon clothes easy:

Plan ahead: Some things—nightwear, bathing suits, and so on —can be chosen right away. For other things, you have to know where you're going.

Be practical: You're going to have to fit your new purchases into your "everyday" life after the honeymoon, so although it's okay to splurge on dressy clothes for your wedding trip, don't overdo it. Instead, look for outfits that can be dressed up or down. For men, this may mean getting a suit you can dress up with a colorful shirt and tie, but which also looks good with a turtleneck sweater for a more casual look.

A woman can change the look of a simple skirt by wearing either a silk blouse or a sporty sweater. Be practical, too, by selecting clothes made from fabrics that don't wrinkle easily and that are easy to clean. Comfort is the most important consideration when choosing shoes. No matter how beautiful they are, shoes that hurt will harm your feet, your back, and your disposition. Shoes that have to be "broken in" should be left in the store.

Stick to two or three complementary colors that can be mixed and matched. This will make packing, dressing, and varying your "looks" easier.

Choose clothes that do "double duty": For instance, if you'll be playing tennis there's no need to buy special tennis clothes. Comfortable shorts and a pullover cotton shirt—both white—will do just fine, and you can use them for other activities. Rubber "shower shoes" serve as bedroom slippers and for the beach or pool. For women, some bra-and-panty sets are beautifully designed and constructed of such sturdy, elastic fabrics that they can be worn as two-piece bathing suits. A lightweight kimono-style bathrobe can be used as a beach cover-up for both men and women.

Travel light: You probably won't need as many clothes as you think—especially if you follow the suggestions in this chapter.

Choose quality over quantity: In other words, acquire fewer clothes but better ones. This requires careful planning, because you'll want to get clothes that go with things you already have. To find out what you really like, if you have a closet full of miscellaneous clothing, take out the items you wear often and hang them up where you can see them. What do they have in common? A color, a type of fabric? You'll want to buy your trousseau clothes to fit in with these favorites. Then take out the clothes you rarely—or never—wear. Give these away to someone else, perhaps to Goodwill or the Salvation Army. They're just taking up space. Also get rid of any shoes that have never been comfortable.

Accessories—jewelry, scarves, ties, hats—are among the best trousseau investments you can make. They can make an inexpensive outfit look better and can dress the same outfit up or down.

Romantic necessities: Don't forget things like sexy underwear for men and women; little odd-shaped cakes of scented soap packed into your luggage that will pleasantly scent your clothes and can then be used for a luxurious bath; a paperback book on massage and a small bottle of body oil; satin sheets, if your hotel or resort doesn't have them; scented bath powder. . . . If you'll be driving (and so, have the space), you might want to take your own pillows and a bottle of champagne.

Perfect Packing

Your trousseau choices will depend, naturally, on where you're going and what you'll be doing, as well as on climate. The following lists don't include every possible option but indicate basics you're likely to need:

LIST #1: THE NECESSITIES OF LIFE

Toothbrush
Toothpaste
Shaving cream
After-shave lotion
Shampoo
Bath oil
Personal hygiene products
Deodorant
Cologne
Perfume
Body lotion
Suntan lotion
Makeup
Fingernail clippers
Emery boards
Nail polish
Nail-polish remover
Mouthwash
Hair conditioner
Tweezers
Bath soap
Packets of detergent
Spot remover
Shoeshine pads
Sewing kit (with safety
   pins)

Razor
Razor blades
Hairbrush
Comb
Travel alarm clock
Travel iron or steam iron
Mirror
Small hair dryer
Camera and film
Portable radio
Transformer (for overseas)
Sunglasses
Umbrella
Sports equipment
Maps/reservations/charts
Passports/driver's licenses
Address book/honeymoon
   notebook
Guidebooks/language phrase
   books
Jiffy towels
Shower cap
Clothesline
Plastic hangers, clothespins,
   bags
Flashlight, extra batteries

Not a Bad Idea to Have on Hand

Pens, pencils
Writing paper
Rubber bands
Bottle opener (corkscrew
   and lift-up types)
Light bulb or small battery-
   operated bed light (foreign bedside lighting is
   apt to be dim)

Scotch tape
Folding raincoat
Washcloth
Jump rope (then you can
   exercise just about anytime
   and anyplace)
Expense record (helps you
   stay within your budget)

LIST #2: CLOTHING

Nightgowns
Pajamas
Bedroom slippers
Light robe
Bathing suit(s)
Beach/pool cover-up
Beach/pool sandals
Dress shoes
Sneakers
Casual shoes
Coat, suitable for climate
Cardigan sweater
Dress
Slacks, casual and dress

Dress skirt
One- or two-piece suit
Shorts
Shirts, casual and dress
Evening wear
Full slip
Half slip
Pantyhose
Socks
Panties and bras
Briefs and shorts
Beach towel
Sports apparel

LIST #3: ACCESSORIES

Sachets or scented soaps
Scarves/bandannas
Belts
Jewelry

Hat(s)
Gloves
Handbag(s)
Ties

Luggage

If your luggage consists of one battered suitcase and a knapsack, this may be the time to invest in a set of luggage that will serve you not only during your honeymoon but for many years and trips to come. If you're starting from scratch, you'll probably choose from the following basics:

· A *train case* or *tote bag* is small enough to fit under a seat or on an overhead rack, but large enough to carry things you might need while traveling or for any overnight stopovers. The case should be no more than twenty-three inches high and nine inches wide.

- A *"weekender"* bag is large enough to hold, as the name implies, two or three days' worth of clothes. If your honeymoon will be spent at a casual place and last no more than three days, the two items listed above, plus a cosmetics case, might be all you'll need.
- A *pullman* (sometimes called a two-suiter or three-suit bag) is large enough to hold up to two weeks' worth of clothes for one person. We like models with full flaps covering each compartment, to keep items from falling out when the bag is opened.
- A *garment bag* holds suits, slacks, and dresses in a hanging position, while other items are tucked around the side. This is one of our favorites because it generally can be carried on an airplane and hung up in a special compartment—this saves waiting for luggage at your destination.

If you expect to be traveling a lot, look for molded luggage with wood or metal reinforcements. These are more likely to survive serious abuse and hard travel than soft-sided bags. Soft-sided luggage has the advantage of being lighter and easier to stuff extra full.

When buying luggage, be sure to handle it in the store. Lift and carry the bag a few steps. Are the handles and the size of the case comfortable? Remember that the case will be significantly heavier when it's full. There should be "feet" on the bottom to prevent wear. Sit the bag down on its feet to see if it's steady. Now examine the outside. Will the bag be easy to clean? Is the material waterproof? Look at the inside and see if the lining and any straps are well sewn. If they aren't it might mean the overall workmanship is poor.

Luggage carriers. While you're looking at luggage, take a look at the luggage carriers. These are folding carts or strap-on wheels that allow you to move your luggage quickly, easily, and without physical strain. Of the two kinds of luggage carriers, folding carts are better. They should be large enough to hold at least one twenty-six-inch suitcase, as well as several smaller suitcases. These carts are a good investment, since they can be used once you're home for moving or shopping.

Packing. Give yourself at least an hour to pack, and use a list of what you'll be taking. Check items off as they're packed. (Use this list again when you're packing to leave for home.) Pack heavier objects such as shoes and portable hair dryer at the bottom of your suitcase (by the hinges), so they won't shift and crush your clothes when the suitcase is carried. Fuzzy sweaters, light-colored clothing, and shoes should be wrapped in individual plastic bags. Belts should be packed around the rim of the case. Fairly wrinkle-free clothes can be folded and then tightly rolled. Place these rolls around the sides of the case along with the belts. Articles such as underwear or socks can be packed inside shoes, boots, or other hollow items. Pack a soft-sided suitcase in your luggage to use for bringing back mementos.

If you'll be going swimming, bring some plastic bags for wet bathing suits. Plastic hangers and clothespins are also useful, for steaming out clothes in the shower, for hanging skirts and pants, and for hanging the laundry. Trial-size samples of cosmetics are perfect for traveling; ask the salesperson for them the next time you're shopping. Use plastic bottles for packing liquids, including medicines. Pack all liquid containers in plastic bags; shaking or changes in air pressure during flying can cause leakage. Chemicals and cigarette lighters should not be packed in your luggage.

It's advisable to pack in your carry-on luggage any glass or other breakable items, cash, jewelry, other valuables or irreplaceable objects, medicines, eyeglasses, and prescriptions. It's also a good idea not to pack more than you can carry by yourself.

On domestic flights, the key to knowing how much you are permitted to take is normally the number of pieces, rather than the weight. On international flights, the weight, size, and number of bags allowed will vary, depending on the airline. No hard-and-fast rules apply, since regulations change constantly.

Most important of all, don't forget to take your luggage—you'd be amazed at how many people do! Either pack it in the trunk of your car *before* the wedding if you'll be driving and leaving that same day, or put it by the door where you can't miss it.

A trousseau is nice to have, but if you can't afford a whole new wardrobe—and who can these days?—just get a few nice things that will make you feel special. After all, the essentials of a happy honeymoon are two loving hearts—and you have those already.

7. PLANNING A FAMILY?

You can't begin too soon to plan your future together, and this planning includes deciding whether—or when—to have a child. Take the time to talk to each other. Discuss both your individual and your combined goals. Ask yourselves questions. For instance, is one or both of you in school or planning to return to school? Do you need two paychecks to get by? Have you a relative close by who might help you if you have a baby? How old and healthy is the relative?

Should You Become a Parent?

Only you can decide whether you want and are capable of caring for children, but one thing is certain: You shouldn't have a child simply because it's expected of you, or in order to hold a marriage together. Nor should you feel ashamed if you decide not to have children. Parenthood is a skill, an art, and a profession, and is not suitable for everyone. A doctor doesn't feel inferior to a lawyer. Nor should you feel inferior if parenting is not where your talents and abilities lie. Would you like to be operated on by a surgeon who was bad at his job but who'd gone into medicine because "Mom and Dad expected it," or "people would've thought there was something wrong with me if I hadn't?" Yet these are just two of the several foolish reasons why people bring children into the world. How will your child or children feel if you commit "parental malpractice" because of such irrational reasons? How will you feel about yourself?

A human life—whether your own or a child's—is important. Plan thoughtfully together, to create the kind of future you want for yourselves.

Most important, does your partner *want* a child? Do you? It isn't enough to feel that having a child is "okay." Having a child you don't want in order to please your mate could be disastrous, not only for you but for the child. The changes a child will make in your life may be felt by you as good or bad, but they *will* be felt. You both have to seriously want a child and be willing to make a huge investment in time, emotions, and money for eighteen years or more.

Another consideration is whether you and your partner actually *like* children. People can be so enraptured with a vision of themselves as the perfect parents of the perfect child that they're unaware of their real feelings—in actuality, they may not like being with real live children for any length of time. So before you have a child, get to know children. Baby-sit for the children of friends and take a child on outings *together*.

Another way of getting to know children is by doing volunteer work—during summer programs; for such children's organizations as the Scouts and Little League; or at a baby or children's health clinic. Find out how well you're able to cope with children who are excited, angry, disturbed, ill, or hard-to-handle—for each of these states is manifested by almost every child at some time. If you feel reluctant to go out of your way to be with children— for instance, to have the child of a friend as a weekend guest— then think how you'd feel having a child as a "guest" for eighteen years!

Even if you both decide you want children, you'll probably want to use birth control to avoid pregnancy during times when choice, poor health, or marital or financial problems make it undesirable. At least you will want to avoid pregnancy until you're both accustomed to your new married life. If you intend to have a large family, birth control should be used to space the children, so that births don't come too close together. *Now* is the time to discuss the birth control options available and to decide which is best for you.

Choosing a Birth-Control Method

There's no such thing as a perfect birth-control method—at various times in your life you may want to use different methods, according to physical health, purpose in using contraception, an esthetic preference, or when new facts about existing methods are found. This doesn't mean that you should change methods whimsically. You should simply reevaluate your needs periodically and make well-thought-out adjustments.

What kind of birth control should you use? That depends on many factors, and a gynecologist or family-planning expert should be consulted. The aspects you'll want to consider in making your choice are (a) effectiveness, (b) safety, (c) side effects, (d) ease of use, and (e) cost. Whatever method you eventually choose, take time to ask questions and do research until you understand fully what the contraceptive does, how it works, and how to use it. People who don't fully understand or feel comfortable with a contraceptive method are likely to use it improperly. If you find you simply don't like a particular method, choose an alternative, but be careful to remain protected while changing methods.

How effective are contraceptives? This varies widely, according not only to the method but also to the people who use it. Studies have shown that couples who are comfortable and matter-of-fact about sexuality, and who discuss it with one another openly, have used contraceptives more consistently and successfully. A stable personality and a stable marriage also contributed to contraceptive success.

The most unsuccessful users of contraceptives were those people who found sex distasteful or frightening, who had sexual and/or marital problems, or who had a pattern of heavy drinking that led to "taking chances." These findings again emphasize the need for communication between husband and wife. The husband can't expect the wife to "take care of it." This is a matter that concerns you both profoundly. It also points up the need for frequent discussions about sexuality and shared responsibility for birth control.

It's a good idea for both of you to have a complete checkup before the wedding; some states require this. It's strongly advised that the woman visit a gynecologist two or three months before the wedding, or immediately if you're already having sexual relations. Before going to the doctor, the woman should write down the age at which she began menstruating; any history of cramps, spotting, missed periods, vaginal infections, pregnancy, or serious illness; and the dates the last period began and ended. If there's a family or personal history of diabetes, heart disease, blood pressure problems, phlebitis (inflammation of veins), or cancer, make note of that, too. If the woman is using oral contraceptives, she should take along the package, plus a list of any other medications she is using.

When choosing a birth-control method, think honestly about yourself. Are you well organized? Impulsive? Are you somewhat squeamish about bodily functions? All these personality factors make a difference, since some methods of contraception require planning and precoital preparation. Your gynecologist should discuss with you the various options available. If he or she simply informs you as to "what you'll use," go see another gynecologist. You need someone who can help you make a thoughtful, rational decision, not someone pushing a "pet" method.

The following is a brief listing of contraceptive methods currently available:

Oral contraceptives, or "the pill," as they are often called, can be highly suitable for young women. For preventing pregnancy, they're the most effective method known, short of sterilization. One tablet is taken every day at approximately the same time for twenty-one consecutive days. After the last pill, nothing is taken for seven days, during which time menstruation occurs. On the eighth day, or the original day of the week on which the pill was first started, the woman begins another cycle or pack of pills ("pilpak"). The woman is therefore on the pill for twenty-one days and off it for seven days, but protection occurs at all times, including the week the woman is off the pill.

Some pills are rigidly packaged with a calendar so that the woman must always begin on a Sunday; still other types have twenty-eight pills in the pack. The pack which contains twenty-eight pills has seven placebos (dummy pills) for the last seven days; the pills are packaged that way so the woman will not get confused and forget to take a pill when she should; she simply takes them every day.

Since no preparation is required before love-making, the pill may be an aesthetically suitable method for people just beginning an intimate relationship. If the pill is started at the correct time relating to the woman's period, it starts being effective after seven days; until then, the couple should either use a backup method such as foam or a condom or else avoid sexual activity.

Despite its important pluses (effectiveness, ease of use, aesthetic qualities), the pill has been under serious scrutiny for many years. Planned Parenthood actively discourages its use for more than five years, and advises that women over thirty-five avoid it completely. Women with a personal history of stroke, phlebitis, impaired liver function, cancer of the breast, estrogen-dependent cancer, heart attack, or high blood pressure should not use the pill; those with a family history of cancer, serious depression, gall-bladder disease, diabetes, or migraine headaches may use the pill only under close supervision. If you're overweight and eat a fatty diet it is discouraged also.

Smoking and the pill, according to recent studies, absolutely do not go together. These studies show that women who smoke a pack of cigarettes a day and take the pill, even if they're under thirty, have an *eight times higher* risk of death by heart attack or stroke. For women over thirty, the risks involved in smoking and taking the pill are extremely high.

There's no general agreement about how long a woman should continue taking the pill. Many doctors recommend that their patients discontinue use for several months every three years to reestablish their natural cycles.

Planned Parenthood cautions that the woman using the pill for five years or longer will have caused at least some permanent damage to her cardiovascular system.

Who should use the pill? If you're under thirty, don't smoke, and intend using it only for the first few years of marriage, it may be for you. Discuss it with your doctor.

Intrauterine devices, usually referred to as IUDs, are small metal or plastic (or a combination of both) objects of various shapes and sizes. The device of your choice is inserted by the doctor through the opening of the cervix into the uterine cavity, where it stays without your feeling it there.

No one knows precisely why IUDs work, but next to the pill, they're the most effective birth-control method available. As with the pill, no pre-lovemaking preparation is needed, so there's no impediment to spontaneity. If you've never been pregnant, you have more chance of suffering the IUDs possible side effects—severe cramps, accidental expulsion (usually when menstruating), and accidental pregnancy. In fact, these side effects are lessened with the newer IUDs. Complications are rare, but serious—perforation of the uterus, pelvic infection, and spontaneous abortion or infection if you become pregnant with the IUD in place.

The effectiveness, safety, and comfort of the IUD seem to vary widely from woman to woman. For this reason, if you have an IUD inserted you should monitor yourself carefully, being alert to any cramping, soreness in the lower abdomen, or unusual bleeding. Despite the negative aspects of IUD use, many women find them safe, effective, and comfortable. Enthusiasm among doctors varies—some feel the data are not really in yet and take a wait-and-see attitude. Others, balancing the risks of pregnancy and childbirth—and the inability of some women to use the pill—consider it a valuable birth-control method.

The diaphragm has become more popular lately among many doctors, who cite its 96 to 97 percent effectiveness if it is used correctly and all the time, and the fact that the diaphragm doesn't affect either the woman's cycle or organs. A molded rubber cap that covers the opening of the cervix and blocks the passage of sperm, the diaphragm reaches that high safety level *only* if used properly. It must be inserted properly, used with a coating of spermicidal jelly to kill any sperm that get around it *every* time you make love, even if you think you're "safe"—and left in for the correct amount of time. If your main concern next to avoiding pregnancy is health, the diaphragm is one of the two most health-preserving methods of birth control. (The exception to this is that in a very small percentage of cases, the diaphragm may cause repeated bladder infections due to pressure on the bladder.) Among the disadvantages are that the diaphragm must be fitted by a physician and may have to be replaced every few years or after childbirth, or gain or loss of ten to twenty pounds or more. It can cause a loss of spontaneity, since the jelly is not effective for more than four hours. Proper insertion may take practice before it becomes quick and easy. Also, the diaphragm must be left in place six to eight hours after intercourse, but not more than twenty-four hours. Because of the pre-planning involved in the use of a diaphragm, it may not be the method of choice for a newlywed, honeymooning couple. It can, however, be a highly desirable choice once the couple has adjusted sexually.

Condoms (sometimes called rubbers) are almost as effective as the diaphragm when used properly. They're readily available without prescription. They give a high degree of protection (although occasional failures result from slippage or puncture) and offer no hazard to the health of either partner. Compact and disposable, condoms offer protection against disease and can actually improve sexual relations by slightly dulling the male's sensations, thereby slowing his progress toward orgasm and allowing lovemaking to go on longer. The disadvantage is that the condom can be felt by both parties. This can be partially overcome by buying those brands which are much thinner and therefore less perceptible. The condom does have to be put on just before making love, but some people make this part of the foreplay, and so don't find it a drawback.

Chemical barriers are generally used as a backup for other types of contraception, such as the diaphragm or condom. They are also used when a pill has been forgotten. However, *aerosol foam* is apparently an effective contraceptive when used *according to directions*—although not as effective as the pill or IUDs. The foam works by both immobilizing and chemically zapping the sperm, and its only adverse side effect is that it can cause irritation and a burning sensation in both males and females.

This varies widely according to brand. No prescription or examination is necessary, and the cost is minimal. The foam is injected into the vagina no more than an hour—preferably fifteen minutes to a half hour—before penetration. A new supply of foam must be injected before each and every act of lovemaking.

Other chemical barriers, such as spermicidal jellies, creams, suppositories, or tablets, are less effective than foam and should be used almost solely as a backup to another method of contraception. They may cause skin irritation because of sensitivity to the chemicals, but no serious health problems.

The rhythm method is used when a couple either can't, or choose not to, use other forms of birth control. With this method the couple abstains from sexual relations during the fertile period—the woman's predicted mid-cycle ovulation day, and three days before and three after. This is one of the two least effective birth-control methods (the other is withdrawal), since its effectiveness depends on the degree of menstrual regularity and the couple's ability to adhere to the "safe" period.

The problems involved with this method are the difficulty of determining the exact time of ovulation, which may vary from cycle to cycle, and the frustration experienced by most people during the times when lovemaking is presumably "not safe." The advantages are its acceptance by the Roman Catholic Church as a method of birth control, and the absence of health hazards. There is no cost, except that of consulting with a gynecologist to try to determine the fertility cycle of the woman involved. Instructions on how to use the rhythm method of birth control can often be obtained at very low cost or free of charge from a family-planning clinic.

Sterilization, while almost 100 percent effective as birth control and entirely free of side effects, should be assumed to be irreversible. It should therefore be chosen only after a great deal of thought. Male sterilization—called vasectomy—has no effect on the normal sexual functioning of the man. It involves cutting and tying off the vas deferens, a duct that delivers sperm to the prostate gland where the semen is formed, and it's usually performed in a doctor's office under local anesthetic or on an outpatient basis in a hospital.

Female sterilization is more complicated, requiring at least a short hospital stay (although a few hospitals or out-patient clinics will release the woman the day of the operation), and it costs more than a vasectomy. In the primary method of female sterilization the fallopian tubes are cut, tied, or sealed so that egg and sperm can't meet. There is no effect on sexual functioning, but as this procedure is complex, serious complications can occur. Any sterilization procedure should be undertaken only after extensive discussion between the couple and their physician, and with a complete understanding of the medical processes involved.

Sharing a Life Together

Your decisions about having a family and choosing a method of contraception will be two of the first and most important of your shared responsibilities in marriage.

This sharing can involve the man helping the woman use a contraceptive device, or involve rotating the total responsibility so that one partner is responsible for a year or so and then the other takes over. The responsibility could shift when the woman goes off the pill every three years, as some doctors recommend, and the husband takes charge of obtaining and using condoms. Or, once a final decision is made to have no more or no children, the couple might consider the sterilization of one partner.

When using contraceptives, follow instructions *to the letter*. Don't feel that accidental pregnancy can't happen to you—it can, and if you're routinely careless about birth control, it eventually will. So act together to make sure you're protected, whenever pregnancy is unwanted.

Section Three

ON THE JOURNEY

8. SETTING THE STAGE FOR INTIMATE MOMENTS

LOVE. Romance. Intimacy. Whatever you call it, it's that extra *something* that makes a honeymoon more than a vacation, whether this is your first, second, or fifth. Even if you'll be camping in the woods, there are so many fun things you can do to make your honeymoon really magic!

"Love notes," said one man when we asked him what had been the most fun on his honeymoon.

"You mean writing each other little messages and hiding them around, or writing sweet things on mirrors with soap, or leaving funny cards. . . ."

"Yeah. Those are great. But I mean on your bodies."

"Bodies?"

"Right. You get body paint and write secret messages on your lover's body—backward! To read the message she has to look in the mirror. And you can have body-painting contests. You each paint the other and take Polaroid shots, and then decide which is best. The winner gets a treat or a little present. Then there's the clean-up detail," he added, rubbing his hands together and grinning wickedly. "You bathe together and make a clean canvas, so to speak!"

A variation on this is to buy some of those bright, glittery colored powders sold in cosmetic or drug stores. Stroked over the body, they give a lovely, unearthly sheen. Used with abandon, it could be messy, though—you'd better plan on leaving an extra tip for the maid who has to clean up. Also, be careful not to get it in your eyes.

Another way to have a "colorful" honeymoon, if you're camping out or if you have a fireplace in your room, is to use a powder you throw on the fire a teaspoon at a time, or special candles that you put under the logs when you start the fire. Both of these make the flames leap with color. You could have a wonderful picnic out in the woods, or even in your hotel room, by a rainbow-colored fire!

If you're picnicking in your room, spread a blanket on the floor and surround yourself with flowers or plants, if possible. In this case you could picnic nude or seminude, and even surround yourself with sensuous sounds via "environmental" recordings of a rainy night, the ocean, or whatever. (You'd have to bring your own cassettes and cassette recorder/player.)

Here's how another young couple spent their first night in their honeymoon hotel:

"We spent the night of the wedding at home and started out the second day, so we wouldn't be completely wrecked when we got to our hotel. This was the smartest thing we could have done —it meant we got there fairly rested. That afternoon we spent finding out what the activities schedule was like, and talking about what we wanted to do the next day. Then we got ready for the Big Night, our real first honeymoon night.

"We'd already decided to have dinner in our room. We had a bottle of champagne delivered with our menus, ordered our dinner, and then sat out on the balcony just sipping and talking and holding hands and getting relaxed. Then we had dinner by candlelight, and a surprise! Rick had hired a guitar player to serenade us! At first I laughed—I was really surprised, and it seemed kind of funny to have this guy just standing out on the balcony, playing love songs for the two of us. Later I almost forgot about him, except for this nice, soft music that was floating in.

"After dinner, the guitar player went away and I went into the bathroom—for the traditional putting-on-the-negligee act, right? Only when I came out I told Rick this was his own private fashion show. He could *look*, but not touch! And I sprung all four of my new negligees on him, doing those model's poses and turns and everything. By the time I got to the last one he was *definitely* romantic!"

No matter what kind of accommodations you have, there are romantic basics you can take along. For the bed, bring along satin sheets if the hotel doesn't supply them, and scatter pot-pourri—a mixture of dried petals of roses or other flowers and spices that you can buy in fancy bath stores or good department stores—inside the sheets. The warmth and moisture from your bodies will release the scent and surround you with fragrance. Bring scented bath powder or a powder-puff mitt, scented lotion, and baby oil.

Perfume can be used in many ways to enhance the romantic atmosphere. For a little titillation the bride can tuck a cotton ball scented with her favorite perfume inside her bra. The cotton ball can also be placed under a pillow. She can add some per-fume to her rinse water when washing underwear. Or splash perfume into her bath water. Another romantic trick is to put a dab of perfume on a light bulb.

You can use basic things in new ways: one bride swears there are *dozens* of sensual uses for shaving cream! A fun—and sexy—activity to do in advance is for both of you to shop for complete sets of sexy underwear. Have your packages gift-wrapped and then model the new items for each other after you get to your honeymoon spot.

You can play love games that will help "break the ice." One game is "Strip 21." You play it just like blackjack or any other way you would like. The basic premise is that whoever wins names two articles of clothing; the loser chooses which one to take off. Another "card" game doesn't have a name, but was de-scribed with great gusto by the man who had apparently in-vented it on his honeymoon. You write down on separate cards whatever sensual/sexual activity turns you on—from being bathed to prolonged kissing to _____! Each person has five to ten cards, and each night—alternating who goes first—the man or woman chooses one card from the other's pack. He or she then performs that activity *immediately!*

How to Striptease

We'll leave the details to your imagination, but for starters we'll give you a few tips:

1. ALWAYS wear high heels—until the *very* end.
2. Wear earrings.
3. Wear several layers of clothing.
4. Direct your audience's eyes by letting your hands linger at selected spots.
5. Accompany with appropriate music, such as Billy Rose's "The Stripper" or Ann Corio's "How to Undress in Front of Your Husband" album.
6. Long black nylons are another must. You wear them as long as you wear the heels.
7. Leave a little something on; remember even Eve left on a fig leaf.
8. Let your husband help.
9. Stay healthy and in good shape.

Never be afraid of being *too* romantic or sentimental on your honeymoon—it's almost impossible! Hide notes containing clues all around the room, one note leading to another until your mate finds his or her little gift. String the bathroom with garlands of red hearts. Hide your watches in a drawer (you can have the operator call you forty-five minutes to an hour before meals or any activities you don't want to miss) so that you get a feeling of timelessness.

Seduce your husband. Seduce your wife. Together, create a time and space in which each of you can express parts of yourself that have to be denied most of the time or with other people. Together, find the part of yourselves that is loving and giving—that longs for unity with another—and nourish it.

9. WHAT ABOUT SEX?

To RELATE and to be aware; to love with mind, heart, and body. These are the things each of us looks for in marriage and which we hope to give to the person we love. To relate means to interact with your mate continuously and as honestly as you can. To be aware is to give full recognition and respect to all the many ways in which your partner communicates with you. And to love with mind, heart, and body is the reason for being wed, for it's almost solely in a good marriage that you can combine every aspect of self in the unifying and fulfilling act of giving yourself to another. Pleasing each other and being loyal to one another isn't part of marriage—it *is* marriage.

Every couple creates their own special balance of all the elements of marriage. In your marriage, sexuality may be more or less important than in the marriages of some of your friends. The balance, too, keeps shifting—sometimes in harmony, so that you barely notice; sometimes during a period of disharmony and readjustment.

Marriage involves a significant readjustment: even if you've made love before, your honeymoon lovemaking will be different. Many people who have lived together before marriage think nothing will change after the wedding. Later, they find that in spite of their preconceptions, being married does make a difference.

Said Tom, a bartender from Arizona:

"When Anne and I decided to get married, it was really to make her parents happy—I didn't think it would make a difference. Well, I was 100 percent *wrong*. It started during the ceremony. Suddenly this was *serious*. I didn't recognize my own voice when I said 'I do.' Then when we got to the hotel where we were honeymooning, and started to make love, I . . . well, I couldn't. For the first time in the two years or so Anne and I'd lived together! I was really shaken. We started talking about it and I finally confessed that the marriage *had* changed things, after all. Anne started laughing and told me she'd been going through the same thing—but she'd been hiding it so she'd be as 'cool' as I was. What a couple of phonies!

"All through the honeymoon we'd mention things that being married changed. Mostly the changes were very minor—things just *felt* different, somehow. And there was something about making love that was different. Not better than before, not worse. Different."

When we're talking about lovemaking, there are no strict guidelines, no absolutes, no guarantees: too many factors enter in. With all the will and love in the world, sometimes learning to make love to the special and particular person you're married to can be a challenge. How we were raised, what ideas we have about sex, our feeling about ourselves as people and as lovers— all influence our lovemaking.

Some people are brought up to think of their sexuality as something other than *them*. These are people who undress in the bathroom and make love only in the dark and who are truly uncomfortable having a serious discussion about sex. Many of us have been exposed to the idea that sex is just not "nice." Yet healthy sexuality (that loving with mind/heart/body) is the giving of pleasure to someone we love—and what could be nicer than that?

Sometimes sexual pleasure can actually be frightening. It can envelop us in sensations that make us feel strange and that, perhaps, we've been taught are "bad" or "dangerous." Sex may become hurried as we try both to possess and avoid the pleasure we crave and fear, so we seek a quick orgasm to release the tension of pleasure. Or we may try to avoid sexual feelings and lovemaking so we don't have to confront our fears.

The honeymoon itself can create problems. The myth is that the newlyweds will suddenly blossom forth into wildly passionate lovers. But if one or both of you is sexually inexperienced, this is not only what you probably *can't* do, but what you probably shouldn't *try* to do. Much happier results are apt to be achieved by a leisurely and loving introduction to sex.

If both of you are fairly inexperienced, you might want to visit a sex counselor together *before* the marriage, to discuss what each of you is expecting and to work through any fears or insecurities either of you may have.

Experienced or not, approach your first night as newlyweds with tenderness and awareness. You aren't there to perform for anyone or to live up to anyone's ideas of sexual prowess, even your own. You're there to begin the long living and loving together that is marriage. Even if the marriage isn't physically consummated that very first night, holding one another, talking, and letting your spouse feel your love is the consummation of your spiritual marriage.

It may take both of you time to become comfortable with sexual feelings and to explore your natural sensuality . . . the pleasures of sight, sound, smell, touch, and taste. But by taking time to savor each sensation, you will discover the tremendous potential your body has for pleasure. Sensuality doesn't relate only to sex. It's a way of interacting with the whole world. Sensuality means being sensitive to your body at all times. Hearing the delicately variable sounds of raindrops striking a window . . . watching the ever-changing sky above . . . relaxing in a scented and warm bath without any thought of the ticking clock . . . these are all sensual experiences. Taking pleasure in one's own sensuality comes before sexual fulfillment.

We're born loving our bodies and loving touching other bodies. We *are* our bodies, but we're taught to "forget" this. We can learn to remember.

The sensuous person doesn't automatically associate touching and being touched with sex, nor does he or she associate nudity with sex. This is harder than it sounds. We've been taught that nudity and sex go together. After all, when do we see people going about their ordinary business without clothes on? Yet the ability to be comfortably nude around your partner at times when you don't want or expect sex is important for a good sex life. Your ability to give freely of your body during sex is directly related to how relaxed you are with your naked body and the naked body of your partner.

If one of you is more shy than the other about nudity, don't badger! Frequent, sincere comments about your partner's attractiveness are much more likely to bring him or her around than nagging (which will probably not only make the shy person more shy, but angry as well!).

Also, if whenever you see your spouse nude you make an immediate sexual pass, you've missed the point. The pleasures of seeing, touching, stroking one another shouldn't be automatic signals that you're going to have sex. Learn to play as a child plays . . . spontaneously, with full regard for whatever pleasures the situation and place offer. Explore your body's capacity for good feelings, and then let sexual expression evolve slowly from this awareness. You have only *this* minute and each succeeding minute in which to be happy. If you wait for happiness in the future (when you have your own apartment? when you get that new job?), it will never come. There *is* no future—only *nows* strung together like beads.

Super-Sex

Almost everyone thinks everyone else is having more and/or better or more varied sex and enjoying it more.

And this isn't surprising. Movies, books, magazines are all telling us about these fantastic—sometimes literally!—sexual experiences: women who have multiple orgasms until they pass out, men who know exotic sexual tricks that ensure them a steady supply of beautiful women at their feet—a wide-screen technicolor sexual extravaganza that makes some of us wonder if our nerve endings were Novocained at birth. Really, we think, our sex is nice, but not like *that*. So what's wrong with us. Or him? Or her?

Nothing—except that we've been misinformed, each sex in a different way. For while there are magazines for women that feature nude photos of men and sexually explicit materials, more young women have been influenced by romantic fiction. In this fiction, the lips of hero and heroine meet and their bodies pulsate and then . . . a fog rolls in or the sound of waves reaches a crescendo, or some such nonsense. The spiritual/emotional content is there and the beautiful agony of just-about-to-be-fulfilled desire, but the subsequent reality—the interaction of two bodies, the graphic description of what goes on sexually—is absent. Of *course* women know what really happens while all the surf is pounding and the fog is rolling in. But at the same time many women expect that sex will somehow not be the physical thing it is—that something mystical will happen.

Young men, meanwhile, have grown up on men's magazines, which, while certainly telling a man everything he needs to know about female anatomy, distort or neglect to tell him what real, day-to-day sexuality with a beloved woman is. He might expect his bride to respond with wild thrashings and jungle noises and a minimum of two orgasms—and feel that his manhood is threatened if she doesn't.

You might say that young women think sex is a mystical experience and young men think sex is a gymnastics exhibition—unless they are unusually enlightened.

In actuality, sex could be more accurately compared to an art or a language. There are physical implements of the "trade"—in this case, your bodies. And there are the nonphysical aspects—a capacity for sensuality, play, and creativity.

Because each long-term love/sex relationship is unique, it can take time to work things out. The more often you touch and are touched by your spouse, the more often you make love, the more comfortable you'll feel and the more your body will respond. Go slowly, gently, and patiently together. Any lengthy sexual relationship will vary wildly in how frequently you make love, how much enjoyment you experience, and the quality of each lovemaking session.

Talking

Sex can be really hard to talk about. For one thing, a lot of us were brought up absolutely *not* to talk about it—or else!

Talking about sex can be especially hard for a woman, but a lot of men have problems communicating verbally about sex, too. You might be afraid of offending or shocking your partner, or of seeming silly or ignorant.

So the two of you should make a mutual-acceptance pact to listen carefully and to accept unconditionally each other's fantasies, desires, and experiences without rejection or judgments. Sometimes it's hard to understand exactly what your lover is trying to say. Often you'll have trouble yourself in putting feelings into words. Since talking about sex in a serious, intimate way may be new, it may take time for both of you to become comfortable with these conversations—all the more reason to make sure that you take the time and arrange to have the privacy for discussions. You can't expect to have one lengthy talk about sex and then forget about it, because both of you will find your sexual desires constantly changing.

How can you begin? You might start by what you've observed: "I notice that when I touch you in certain ways you seem to tense up—am I doing something you don't like?" or, "You really seemed to like what we did tonight." This kind of opener is natural for just after you've made love, when you're holding each other and feeling close.

If this seems impossible for you right now, you may have to schedule a time for talking. Yes, scheduling a time for talking about sex can feel uncomfortable and unnatural. But so does holding a tennis racket for the first time, or changing your eating habits. You might especially need to schedule a time for talking about sex if ordinarily you just "never get around to it." People who have difficulty communicating about sex or other intimate feelings may fill their time together with work, friends, projects, hobbies, recreations, children—anything and everything that will save them from taking the risk of talking about their most intimate feelings. Television is perhaps the greatest bar to intimacy we have—two people are together, but not communicating at all. So at least once a week turn off the television, take the phone off the hook, and *talk*.

Problems, Problems

As one wit has observed, you can worry about anything, given the determination!

The facts are that most men can be impotent, premature ejaculators, or nonorgasmic once in a while. And most women can be frigid, nonorgasmic, or uninterested in sex once in a while.

The real danger in such situations is that we'll worry about them so much that the problem becomes worse. Just remember that work, health, or family problems can interfere with sexual response and pleasure, and that your sexual satisfaction and performance will improve as these other conditions improve. The time to think seriously about getting professional help is when, even with patience and loving help from your spouse, the problem continues longer than, say, a month or so.

One more "problem" that should be mentioned is that of sexual boredom—the dread "blahs!"

Generally speaking, the causes of the "blahs" can be assigned to one of the three following groups:

Lack of communication: you have a much, much better chance of enjoying the sort of sexual activity you want if you *ask* for it! And if your spouse consistently does something that turns you off, you should let him or her know about that, too (tact, of course, is called for here!).

Unspoken anger: another communication problem, anger that you keep to yourself (a silent grudge), will begin by destroying your capacity for sexual response and will eventually turn your partner off as well. This unspoken anger can also reveal itself verbally, but in a sneaky way. "Gee, sweetheart, you sure are clumsy" (or other, often worse, comments) seem to come naturally, and your spouse becomes angry at you. There's something to be said for a good, clean fight, but stick to the immediate incident that brought on your anger. Fights that enlarge endlessly to include all grudges going back five or ten years are hugely destructive.

Too much togetherness: surprise, surprise, but that is exactly what Dr. Jay Kuten, assistant professor of psychiatry at the

Boston University School of Medicine, believes is responsible for many cases of sexual boredom. He asserts that while togetherness and time spent together sensually and sexually lead to good sex, too much of the same has the opposite effect!

The more individuality each partner possesses, Kuten says, the better the sex should be. And, if all else fails, try a good fight: "Anger and its shared expression in fighting happens to make the loving and the lovers new again. This alternation of feeling and action, of loving and hating, works to keep things honest within the relationship, to keep the lovers real to one another and whole to themselves." Dr. Kuten warns, however, that constant bickering will have the opposite effect.

Counseling

There is some wisdom in seeking premarital sex counseling in order to spot problems that may occur in your marriage and to learn how to deal with them before they get out of hand. The cost for such counseling can range from nothing to around $50 per session.

How to find a counselor?

The counselor doesn't necessarily have to be a professional. An understanding religious adviser or family doctor might answer many of your questions. If, however, you feel you have potentially serious sexual problems, you probably should go to a professional. This might be a psychologist or psychiatrist specializing in sexual counseling. Your county Mental Health Association can provide counseling (at a rate in proportion to your income) and can also refer you to professionals in your area. Another source is the American Medical Association: it won't recommend a particular person, but will refer you to qualified people in your area. If you have a friend or relative who knows of someone, you can ask him or her. If your "problem" with sex is simply inexperience, you may solve part of it by reading some of the excellent books on sexuality that are available.

Marriage is an intricate relationship in which each person

communicates and gives to the other intellectually, emotionally, physically, and, some would say, spiritually. Sex isn't the most important ingredient in a good marriage, but it does count, and it can make a *good* marriage *great*.

Fun & Fancy

The Bridegroom:

Upon His Spouse Locking Herself in the Bathroom
for Two Hours on Their Wedding Night . . .

. . . *the shy bridegroom* will try to fall asleep before she comes out;

. . . *the daring bridegroom* will try to have a brief but meaningful relationship with the chamber maid;

. . . *the polite bridegroom* will write all the thank-you notes and sign his bride's name;

. . . *the humorous bridegroom* will booby-trap the room with practical jokes;

. . . *the passionate bridegroom* will knock on the bathroom door every sixty seconds and ask when she'll be out;

. . . *the cold bridegroom* will go over his tax return again to see if the IRS owes him money after all;

. . . *the serious bridegroom* will use this time to brush up on medieval German;

. . . *the nervous bridegroom* will bite his fingernails and toenails to the quick;

. . . *the neat bridegroom* will remake the bed until it's perfect;

. . . *the sociable bridegroom* will invite the entire Elks convention in for a surprise party for his bride;

. . . *the lazy bridegroom* will watch TV fully clothed, waiting
for his bride to come out and undress him;

. . . *the energetic bridegroom* will exercise until the room
smells like a locker room after a football game;

. . . *the creative bridegroom* will take apart the furniture and
make an avant-garde sculpture;

. . . *the frightened bridegroom* will hide under the bed
hoping she'll forget all about him;

. . . *the understanding bridegroom* will write love letters on
hotel stationery and slip them under the bathroom door
every half-hour. . . .

The Bride:

*Upon Finding Out Her Husband's Snores Sound Like
a Jack-hammer in an Echo Chamber* . . .

. . . *the scientific bride* will chart his snores on a seismograph
and find that they rate as high on the Richter scale as the
second most severe earthquake ever to hit China;

. . . *the sentimental bride* will tape-record the snores so she
can play them whenever her husband is away;

. . . *the sociable bride* will invite passersby in for a snore
concert;

. . . *the tired bride* will crawl off to sleep in the closet;

. . . *the passionate bride* will stop his snores by waking him
up and giving him something more interesting to do;

. . . *the humorous bride* will sit up all night writing snore
jokes;

. . . *the polite bride* will ignore them if it kills her, and it may;

. . . *the moody bride* will reflect gloomily that if he *really*

loved her he would have given her a year's worth of
earplugs as a wedding present;

... *the serious bride* will review in her mind every word she's
read in the last twenty years about snoring;

... *the independent bride* will call the desk and get them to
give her a separate room;

... *the nervous bride* will get tense every time he skips a
snore;

... *the good-natured bride* will reflect that a good man's
snores can be the sweetest kind of music. . . .

10. GETTING TO KNOW
ONE ANOTHER

A HONEYMOON is a chance to get away from daily chores and
everyday living, a vacation from our ordinary lives. And yet
there is one thing we can't take a vacation from—ourselves. Our
unspoken expectations of what our husband or wife will be like
now that we're married, our assumptions about what married life
will do for us, go right along with us wherever we go.

For instance, one partner may somehow believe that the
other will stop disagreeing with his or her opinions in public
now that they are married, even though he or she might have
admired such outspokenness before. Then, during their first
dinner at the honeymoon resort, they begin talking about politics
with another couple and one partner disagrees with the other.
The newlywed is shocked! It's like being hit with a grenade.
Without knowing why, he or she is *furious.*

The fact is that even though we may have grown up closely

observing two fallible, imperfect human beings engaged in matrimony (our parents), we still have some highly idealized and completely unrealistic ideas of what marriage is going to do for us. "We're never, ever going to quarrel the way Mom and Dad did," thinks she. "Now that we're married, I'll never feel lonely," he thinks.

It would be nice if all the difficult adjustments marriage brings could be put off until after the honeymoon. But unfortunately, as soon as we marry, a switch clicks in our heads and all our illusions come forward like a line of little soldiers. If we don't confront them, they can shoot down a potentially good marriage or at least provide a troubled beginning.

It's even possible that one or both of you might behave badly on your honeymoon. This is a reaction to the stress of the wedding, travel, and new and unsettling, even if pleasant, places; of being intimate emotionally and physically with another person; and of having fears about the consequences of marriage. The reactions can go to either extreme—withdrawal or outrageous flirtation with others; fits of temper or bouts of lethargy. One bride spent her entire honeymoon weeping and hiding in the hotel room—but she's now been very happily married for more than ten years.

Does all this unhappy stuff *have* to happen? There's really no telling. If you have absolutely no problems or disappointments on your honeymoon, wonderful! It's delightful when reality lives up to expectations. It's when things don't go right that you might need advice.

A marriage is very much like an ocean—sometimes stormy and sometimes becalmed, with troughs and waves, always moving and changing. Wouldn't it be dull otherwise? We're all loving and cold, selfish and giving, loyal and treacherous. Easy to say, but the first time your new husband or wife shows the negative side of his or her personality, it can be as much of a shock as finding a tarantula in your shoe. How did it get there?!

So long as you don't throw in the towel or throw up your hands and stomp off, all these disagreements and problems can actually make your marriage better, happier, more romantic, and more fulfilling! Too much closeness, compatibility, and agreeableness adds up to Cream of Wheat. Yes, Cream of Wheat is yummy—added to a diet of spiced foods and even some "junk" food now and then.

Those nasty little shocks about each other at least bring home the point that this person you've promised to love and cherish is a real, live, changing personality. This doesn't alter the fact that when you're really angry you could just kill him! Or, maybe, call up that old girl friend of yours (the one she's wildly jealous of) just to say "Hi." Having problems doesn't necessarily mean you have a rotten marriage. It could mean you have an intimate marriage—warts, roses, and all.

Marriage counselors say that much of the excitement (good and bad) between a couple will diminish. The romance and the disagreements will slowly lessen and the couple will become as much friends as lovers. So if comfortable, friendly, lasting love is what you want, the only way to get to it is through all the problems and upheavals of early marriage.

A Time of Adjustment

If you've ever read any of those wildly romantic novels, you may have noticed that the book ended when the mystery and crisis ended and the lovers were madly passionate for one another. But what, oh what, will they do now that they're married, and no longer threatened by death or a fate even worse?

No magic formulas exist to ensure that your marriage will succeed. But you can follow certain suggestions that will contribute to a successful life together. Make a commitment to your marriage; work at it just as you work at your job or at acquiring a particular skill. Grow and change together. If you notice that you're growing at different rates, talk about how you can make your rates mesh together.

No relationship is perfect; problems are bound to arise. When they do, don't be the proverbial ostrich and stick your head in the sand. Face any problem squarely and quickly. Tackle it as soon as you recognize its existence.

Chances are, you're each going to be unhappy about one or

two things you learn about your mate. A person capable of one hundred-percent acceptance of another has yet to be found. Also, you may be feeling extra-critical toward your new spouse. This is a way of backing off a little from what, right now, may feel like too much closeness, and it will pass. You also may begin feeling too critical about yourself, wondering when she'll notice that you're really a klutz, or when he'll notice that your thighs are really horribly chubby. This too will pass.

During this time of adjustment and change you may find all sorts of anxieties or doubts bobbing to the surface of your mind. Among them:

Fear—not waking-up-in-the-middle-of-the-night dreads, but the sneaking, skin-crawling little anxieties that can cause even a person deeply in love to behave oddly. Worries about the loss of freedoms, the consequences of marital commitment, or of your partner changing can nibble away at your happiness, yet you might hesitate to bring these up. He/she might think you're not really in love or that you're silly.

Now is the time to begin talking to each other, even if you're uncomfortable. Odds are that as soon as you've finished talking about *your* fears, your partner will reveal his (or hers). Both men and women fear losing their freedom, privacy, and independence. If you talk about your fears together, you can reassure each other that these fears are groundless and can make plans which will ensure that neither partner loses valuable aspects of his or her premarital self.

Honeymoon myths can get you worried when you really don't have to be. For instance, we've been talking about having problems adjusting to a new relationship while on your honeymoon; if you do have these problems, it doesn't mean you'll have them throughout your marriage. Just about anything could go wrong on your honeymoon, but if you are flexible and have a sense of humor you'll live through it and even have a few laughs. A resort in the Poconos asked its newlywed guests about funny things that happened on their wedding night. Here are some of the answers:

"My wife got up at 3:30 in the morning and decided to iron some clothes."

"*He* got stuck in a revolving door with all our luggage!"

"Our friends put stones in the hubcaps as a joke, and after we stopped to get them out we spent about two hours trying to get the hubcaps back on the car. We pounded and shook the car so hard, the cork popped out of our champagne and sprayed the inside of the car. We had our first fight on the way to the resort and refused to talk to each other. When we got to the bus station, where we were to get final directions to the resort, it was 3 A.M. and no one was there to meet us. I was still angry, but so scared that we became friends again!"

If you get homesick on your honeymoon, something's really wrong! Right? *Wrong.* Some longing for the familiar is only natural, especially during this monumental change in your life.

If you aren't super-passionate there's something wrong—after all, everyone else is! This is another common misconception. Some people don't get off the ground sexually until things have settled down. And it's quite possible that a couple who start off slowly will have a better-than-average sex life later.

You might think there's something wrong if you feel a let-down on your honeymoon. Well, think about it: you've been dashing around madly, fulfilling your responsibilities at home and at work, arranging the marriage and honeymoon and having a fuss made over you. Now, all at once, you're far from home and the racing about is over. Things can seem to come down with a thump. But once the noise and running are over, you can quiet down and talk to this person you've married.

One last myth is the idea that you'd better live it up now, because soon the honeymoon will be over! But why? This isn't going to be the last trip you ever take, and your lives aren't going to be all that dull later on. There's really no reason to drive yourselves into exhaustion by rushing into absolutely every activity, by drinking too much and sleeping too little.

Close, Closer, Closest

Sometimes we truly love and cherish another person and yet have trouble letting him or her know about it on a day-to-day basis. After all, we'd feel silly vowing our love each hour on the hour, and the words would pretty soon turn to cardboard. How can you get closer and at the same time express your love?

Confide in your mate and allow him or her to confide in you. Listen without interrupting, and then repeat in your own words what your partner has just said. Sometimes you shouldn't say anything at all, but only listen sympathetically. And when you need to confide in someone, choose your spouse. It might be hard to talk to him or her about something you find embarrassing or sad or angering, but by confiding your human feelings, you allow your spouse to do the same.

Share the little things, the funny-looking dog you saw, a joke someone told you. Some people think they'll bore the other person, but marriage is made up of small things.

Talk, talk, talk—and then shut up. One of the hardest things to learn (unless you know it by instinct) is the art of when to speak and when to be silent. Talking is extremely important, since it's the only way our partner is going to find out what we're thinking and feeling. Mind-reading ability doesn't come with a marriage license. Expecting the other person to somehow "know" what's going on in your mind is immature. If you have a fight, keep it clean—no really mean personal attacks, but an airing of issues; it will make you closer. Anger bottled up turns from hot to cold and freezes love.

Touch, when talking isn't the right thing to do. Some people just naturally show their feelings physically. Touching your partner's hand, taking each other's arm as you walk, stroking his or her shoulders, can be more satisfying than—and certainly as valid as—daily passionate avowals of love.

Problems and Solutions

There are certain subjects that experts say are common sources of marital arguments. You might consider talking about these ahead of time—before they become problems. Forewarned, you can begin to recognize what can and cannot be changed. Or finally, when problems do crop up, as they undoubtedly will, you can be assured that you aren't the only couple in the world experiencing difficulty. Key areas to be wary of are money, division of chores, visiting friends, and each other's relatives. Others include smoking, drinking, overeating, and other personal habits; changing attitudes; and a general lack of communication. People also tend to argue over past events, disappointments, and regrets.

Often, it's the little things that drive us bonkers: the razor stubble in the sink, the overflowing ashtrays, whatever. Things that are so little and, really, so unimportant, that we feel silly complaining. And yet they *bother* us. How to handle little annoyances?

Remember you aren't perfect either, so there are bound to be little things you do that annoy your partner and that you might not even be aware of. Give each other the benefit of the doubt. He may not know that his stubble is making you crazy; she may not be aware that you hate overflowing ashtrays. Keep things in perspective: some of these little annoyances are indeed unimportant, and are things you can learn to live with. Neither of you is a clone of the other—you can't always do things in the same way.

So look at your own attitude. Is his or her behavior really annoying? Or are you sort of annoying yourself by thinking it should be done *your* way?

What truly drives you bananas? We mean something you've tried to adjust to but that still makes you grind your teeth. You do have a right to ask your spouse to change behavior that's significantly annoying and inconsiderate.

Come right out with your feelings. It's no use waiting for your mate to figure out what throws you into a sulk. You'll just have to tell him or her. Simply, and without anger or guesses as to the "motivation" of the annoying behavior, talk about the behavior. But be careful to address the *behavior*—not your spouse. If you say, "You're really selfish. Every time we're going out you make me run around finding things for you and helping you get ready. You don't care that I have to get ready too, you're only thinking of yourself . . ." and so on, this is guaranteed to begin a bitter argument. Approaching it like this: "I don't think you realize that when I spend so much time getting you ready,

I can't get myself ready, and this means we're usually late. Think we can solve this problem?" seems more likely to begin a discussion of how to find a solution for the problem.

Have alternatives ready: "We could start getting ready earlier, or I could help you get organized in the afternoon so you won't need me later."

Make your way attractive: Appeal to your partner's logic, ego, sense of fair play. Point out that if he or she does *this* (gets ready to go out without your help), you'll do *that* (resolve to put an end to your lateness).

Compromise: Give a little, get a little—and vice versa. Share the task of getting used to one another by being as sensitive to your mate's feelings and needs as you want him/her to be toward yours. Play nice—and play fair.

The Great Honeymoon Cake Fight

A young man named Tower
Used all of his power
To get a young woman named Kate
To bide by his wishes
To do all his dishes
In other words, share all his fate.

The couple were happy
And, blessed by her pappy,
Took leave on their sweet honeymoon
With bells and with jangles
With laces and bangles
They set off from home around noon.

But then they got quarrelsome
And fearsome and brawlsome

(They fought all the way in the car.)
And when they got where they
Intended to stay they
Proceeded to go to the bar.

The marriage was ended
Before it began-ded.
The onlookers blushed with chagrin,
Until a stout fellow
Proceeded to bellow
Demanding an end to the din.

"Look here, you two lovers,
You know there are others
Who're still in the honeymoon mood.
So why not a duel,
If you must be foo-els
And let the duel weapon be—food!!!

Hearts full of ire,
Eyes bright with fire,
The newlyweds walked to the lake.
They pushed up their sleeves,
Stood flexing their knees
And called for their weaponry—cake!

They tossed it and mashed it,
They trampled and bashed it
—A wedding cake, symbol of hope—
Then after a while
They both had to smile:
They found that they just couldn't mope.

He stood there and sighed
At his cake-covered bride

With icing all over her hair
And thought that there'd never,
Never been *ever*
Such a ridiculous pair.

The crowd then applauded.
They certainly lauded
This end to the honeymoon strife.
The cake was demolished
But anger abolished
And husband united with wife.

Since then through the years
Through laughter and tears
They've dueled the very same way.
They've found love's kept bright
With a once-yearly fight
With *cake* each anniversary day!

---

11. MAKING MEMORIES

NEVER underestimate the power of memories. When you're happy, they accentuate the mood; when you're blue, they can remind you of past happiness and give you the hope that that happiness will come again. An old matchbook cover, a tattered pressed flower, a cork from a champagne bottle, or even the cap from the first tube of toothpaste you shared can bring loving memories rushing back.

Save all the things you might think are silly to save—drink

stirrers, napkins, or matches with the names of clubs or restaurants you visited; postcards; the bride's garter and the bridegroom's boutonniere; a lock of both the bride's and bridegroom's hair; a newspaper from the day you were married; a television guide the first night you *didn't* watch TV.

Other special ways of preserving fleeting moments are simple, inexpensive, and highly personal. You can soak the edges of a wedding invitation with after-shave or cologne, date the card as to where and when this was done, and seal it in a waxed or cellophane envelope. If you're using a guidebook, jot down your impressions and experiences in the margin, or on slips of paper you can insert between the pages. Buy a record of a song that's popular during your honeymoon time and which means something to you.

Write love letters to each other, then seal and keep them to be opened and read for the first time on your first anniversary; at that time, write others to be opened on your second, and so on.

Be aware of what's special to *you*, and use your imagination.

You might buy one of those bound books with blank pages and use it as a combination honeymoon diary (which you both write in each evening) and autograph book—get the waiter who serves you your first married meal, the social director, or friendly people you meet to write a short message and sign their names.

Ask the waiter or manager of a restaurant or bar for an ashtray or a menu—when you tell them you're honeymooners and that you want it as a remembrance of the wonderful time you had at their establishment, they aren't likely to turn you down! Just be sure not to "liberate" anything, that is, take it without asking.

You've probably had rolls and rolls of pictures taken at the wedding, with you two as the "stars." Now that you're on your honeymoon, take care to remain the stars. A picture of a beautiful beach or a quaint house is a hundred times more meaningful and interesting if you're both in the frame. Luckily, you don't have to buy the world's most expensive and complicated camera to get photos that include you both and are sharp and clear. Any moderately priced camera can be used with an inexpensive tripod and timer—with these, you don't have to rely on a kindly stranger to snap the shot, and you can also get more intimate pictures.

On the subject of strangers, if you're interested in taking someone's picture and that person is aware of what you're doing, always ask if he or she minds. Most likely he or she won't, but it's good manners to ask anyway. (Also, in some countries, locals believe that being photographed is bad luck.)

Some hints on getting better-than-average pictures:

- Take three times more pictures than you think you'll want; professional photographers take several rolls in order to get a few good prints.
- Keep your camera loaded and ready for those unexpected opportunities to get an unusual shot.
- Try to have people *doing* things in your pictures—the person weighing the fish at an outdoor market, say, or children climbing on a statue.
- Think of telling a story with pictures. For instance, at a fishing village you might want a few shots of the boats coming in, the fish being unloaded, the marketplace, and then the person weighing the fish.
- Look for the interesting angle. Walk around whatever it is you want to photograph. Look at it from higher up and from the ground level. Think about whether the object would be more interesting in a close-up, medium shot, or from a distance. For instance, a large statue might be more interesting in your picture if you choose to take a close-up of part of it, rather than photographing the whole.

Once you've taken your pictures, there are many fun and unusual things you can do with them. You can have picture-buttons made, T-shirts, large poster-size blowups, computer pictures. . . . You may want to have some enlargements made and cut out pieces of them to mount together into a collage.

You can also have a different sort of picture made of the two of you. A charcoal or chalk sketch, silhouettes, or copper-stencil portraits can be inexpensive and decorative.

Fabulous memories can be made using one of the new super-easy video cameras—your own or a rented one. The newest ones are ready to replay within ninety seconds.

Photographs are an immortalization of your physical selves, and tape recordings can preserve your voices, feelings, and thoughts. You can add greatly to your memorabilia by recording local sounds, such as a foghorn, trolley bell, street musicians, or an orchestra or band playing "your" song. Use the recorder as a sort of diary made in sound. To do this, make sure that the tape machine you get is a recorder as well as a player. Cassette types (or the mini-cassettes) are usually preferred because they're small and easy to use. Almost all recorder/players can be used either with batteries or electricity. Many have built-in microphones, so that you don't have to bother with the hand-held kind.

Once you become accustomed to your portable tape recorder, you'll discover all kinds of fun to have with it. You can "interview" your relatives and friends before and after the wedding, interview strangers—or new friends—while on the honeymoon, and end each day with a short spoken diary entry by each of you. Just be sure you buy the best brand of tape you can afford. The "bargain" brands are no bargain—they're too full of hissing noises.

When considering the subject of souvenirs, try coming up with one or two "rules" that you'll both agree to follow. Most souvenirs cost little or nothing—pebbles from the beach, photographs, matchbooks. But there probably will be things you'll want that *do* cost money. If you haven't agreed on a budget in advance, you may find that buying one little thing after another adds up shockingly. So decide first off how much you're going to budget for souvenirs, and try very hard to stick to this.

Your second consideration should be whether you can get the same item for about the same cost closer to home—it doesn't make such sense to buy something in a resort town that you could just as easily get down the street at home. When buying souvenirs try to choose things that reflect the place where you're buying them—a shell necklace from Jamaica or wood carvings from Africa or a paperweight model of the Statue of Liberty if you're honeymooning in New York City. If possible, get items that are useful or decorative or both—not something that'll end up in the back of a drawer once you're home. If you can afford it, you may want to buy one or two expensive souvenirs that you expect to become more valuable as time goes by.

Finally, no matter where you go outside of the U.S., you must be sure of what you can and can't bring back into the country with you. You'll also need to take into account the amount of duty you'll have to pay. The government allows a generous amount per person, duty free. When you buy anything overseas, in Canada, or in Mexico, be sure to keep your sales slip to show the customs officer. The U.S. Customs Office publishes a booklet spelling out its regulations. If you're going abroad, be sure to get this booklet and read it through before you make any purchases. You will find the address necessary for obtaining this booklet, as well as lots of other practical addresses, in Part Two of this book.

12. THE FOOD OF LOVE

It all began with Adam, Eve, and the apple—and food and lovers have been inseparable ever since. The honeymoon itself supposedly evolved beginning around 400 B.C., when newly married couples drank mead (a fermented drink made from honey) for the first thirty days after their wedding, probably for fertility and luck. And feasting has always been the most popular way of celebrating a marriage.

Many wedding customs—such as showering the happy pair with rice (in India and America), wheat (France), or raisins, figs, and dates (Morocco)—involve food as a symbol of fertility, good fortune, and happiness.

Throughout history most great lovers, from Cleopatra to Casanova and DuBarry to Don Juan, have also been great eaters, seeking magical potions and elixirs which would arouse the passions of their beloved.

In mythology, aphrodisiacs (by definition foods or drugs that stimulate or intensify desire) were first concocted by Aphrodite, who was, appropriately, the Greek goddess of love. She stimulated the ardor of her companions on Mount Olympus with ambrosia and nectar. Although her contribution to the art of seduction has been debunked by literal-minded skeptics, many a lover still believes in the wisdom of Aphrodite and takes to heart the adage "The way to a man's heart is through his stomach."

Although modern scientific research has been unable to prove that there are foods which really do turn a reluctant lover into an amorous partner, aphrodisiac pantries are still well stocked. Among those cultures which tout the sexual powers of certain foods are the Chinese, French, Italian, and Latin American. In some Arab countries, a snack consisting of twenty almonds and one hundred grains of pine nuts plus a glass of honey is said to increase the sexual appetite when consumed three nights in a row. The Chinese favor ginseng as a sexual stimulant, and the French swear by truffles.

In ancient Greece, carrots were called *philons* (*philo* meaning "loving") and were always included in the seducer's culinary offerings. Aristotle is said to have used peppermint as an aphrodisiac, and Pliny whipped up some hyena eye with a dash of dill and licorice to heighten his passions.

Dill was also a favorite of European lovers during the Middle Ages. They produced a love potion by steeping dill in wine. Sesame seeds are another flavoring said to possess sexual qualities. One recipe called for soaking them in beaten-up sparrow eggs and then cooking them in milk.

Cheese too is considered a symbol of love, strength, and fertility. Swiss cheese originated because there was a custom that when a daughter was born, a "wheel of romance" was placed in a cave and not removed until her wedding day, when it became the focus of her wedding feast.

Seafood—especially oysters, shrimp, lobster, and crab—has always been exceedingly well regarded as an aid to lovemaking. Before indulging in their favorite pursuit, both Casanova and Lord Byron were reported to have consumed enormous quantities of seafood.

Apples are favored by lovers for more than keeping the doctor away! Although you might not care to try this, an ancient German superstition holds that eating an apple soaked in the sweat of your lover's armpits will increase love. By the way, not all cultures agree that apples were the forbidden fruit of Eden. Moslems, for instance, say a banana was the culprit that got Adam and Eve turned on and out.

Eggs have been popular as an aphrodisiac throughout the ages, either eaten raw or combined with other foods such as asparagus, which was boiled in a sauce made with spiced egg yolks. Caviar (fish eggs) is an all-time favorite.

Other foods and condiments which have been touted as sexual turn-ons include tomatoes (called "love apples" by the French), avocados, onions, artichokes, ripe olives, pomegranates, figs, garlic, cinnamon, curry powder, parsley, cloves, and rose hips.

"To heat the blood, quicken the senses, strengthen the muscles, and thereby rouse up, provoke, excite, and enable vigorous accomplishments of amorous dalliance," alcohol has been put to use for just about as long as there have been people.

Champagne, of course, is the queen of love drinks: Madame Pompadour called it "the only wine that leaves a woman beautiful after drinking it." However, sherry (Spain), sake (Japan), and beer (Germany) are among other favored beverages. Also, many a would-be lover has concocted his or her own special "love potion" to ensnare the object of ardor. During their honeymoon in the Poconos, the "Honeymoon Capital of the World," newlyweds have been known to consume as many as one hundred goblets of the "Pocono Love Potion"—a special beverage whose recipe remains a well-guarded secret.

While alcohol *does* loosen inhibitions, too much is a definite impediment to lovemaking—what could be worse than having so much to drink that you don't remember what fun you had . . . or awaken with a dreadful hangover! One wit observed (and we agree) that the seven stages of drunkenness are "verbose, grandiose, amicose, bellicose, morose, stuperose, and comatose . . . and lovers had best stop at the third stage."

As you may have noticed by now, there's hardly any food, beverage, or spice that hasn't been promoted as love-enhancing at one time or another. And although there doesn't seem to be a *physical* effect from aphrodisiacs, there is a psychological effect. A romantic setting, a meal made up of foods you don't have on an everyday basis, and—most important—two people in love create an atmosphere that in itself is a potent aphrodisiac!

If you'd like to select your own special "love feast" during your honeymoon, you'll find plenty of choices on almost any menu. For breakfast you might order an omelette with caviar and sour cream, along with generous helpings of strawberries in champagne (one of our own favorite combinations any time of day or night).

For lunch, a "love apple" (tomato) stuffed with crabmeat salad, followed by peaches poached in wine, should set your amorous juices flowing. At dinner, an appetizer of oysters Rockefeller gets things off to a good start. You could follow with a shish kebab of lamb, broiled chicken breast, or filet mignon served with asparagus and an avocado-and-mushroom salad. Top this off with a sumptuous, gooey chocolate dessert or fruit and cheese. Casanova couldn't have asked for more!

On the other hand, love food can be as simply delightful as marshmallows toasted over a crackling fire, mugs of rich hot chocolate with a stick of cinnamon, or the traditional "a loaf of bread, a jug of wine, and thou." The idea is to enjoy food as part of your personal sensuous honeymoon experience (and afterward, too)!

Perhaps this bit of ancient advice best sums up our ideas of aphrodisiacs and love potions:

I shall show you a love philtre without medicaments, without herbs, without a witche's incantations. It is this: If you want to be loved, love.

Section Four

TO SMOOTH THE JOURNEY

13. DINING OUT

ONE of the most enjoyable parts of your honeymoon may be the chance to eat out more than usual and try new and different foods. This is especially true if the area in which you're honeymooning is famous for its local cuisine—Mexican, Creole, Amish, or whatever. Try to sample the famous local dishes, wines, and desserts, and collect recipes so that you can re-create those dishes you enjoyed most once you get home.

If there isn't any particularly distinctive style of cooking in the area where you're staying, you might find interesting ethnic restaurants to explore. Even if you have a meal or two that isn't entirely satisfactory because of its strangeness to you, you'll discover many more that are delicious. In some areas you'll be able to find unusual places to dine, such as with a local farm family or in a plantation restaurant. If you want to dine alfresco, you can call room service and order a picnic lunch—expect to pay extra for this, though. Remember also that if you've paid a package price for your accommodations (that is, if your room price includes meals), you won't get credit for any meals eaten out.

You can find out what an area offers in the way of cuisine by consulting your travel agent or friends before you leave or by looking at food and travel magazines or local newspapers or magazines. If the impulse strikes and you'd just like to eat out, you may ask whoever's at the front desk to recommend a restaurant (beware, though—they may not really know the good restaurants, or may send you to a place just because it's run by a friend or because they get a commission from the owner).

To ensure that exploring new foods and restaurants is a pleasant experience, here are a few guidelines:

Reservations, credit, and dress: You'll want to make reservations for any but the most casual restaurants, especially for a

Friday, Saturday, or holiday. When you call for your reservation, ask if the restaurant accepts your particular credit card, if you expect to pay that way. To avoid embarrassment, check on the dress requirements at the club or restaurant you're planning to visit—being turned away hungry is a miserable experience you don't need.

Coat check: You can check your coats, or keep them with you and let them hang over the backs of your chairs. It's courteous for a woman to assist a man with his coat, just as he should help with hers. It is advisable to keep fur coats with you.

Ordering: If you need a special diet, explain this quietly to the waiter (without going into great detail) and be specific in placing your order: "No salt." "Is there sugar in this dish?" Repeat the order to make sure it's understood. At a resort, you may want to write ahead with specifics or speak with the chef on the day you arrive. If your dietary needs are of special importance—as in the case of diabetes, for instance—don't be shy about firmly making sure these needs are met. Just be sure to notify the persons concerned well ahead of time.

If you can't get the waiter's attention, wait until he or she is near your table and simply say "Waiter" or "Waitress." You may also ask another attendant to send your server to you. If you're kept waiting for service an unreasonably long time, get your waiter's attention and quietly but firmly ask for an explanation, or go to the captain—or leave. Remember, you're there to enjoy—not upset—yourself. If there's a problem in the kitchen, or if a certain dish requires extra preparation time, the waiter should let you know when you place the order.

If your dining time is limited because of other plans, tell the waiter as soon as you're seated so your meal can be served as quickly as possible. On the other hand, if you want to take your time, let the waiter know you're not in a hurry and want to rest between courses.

If there's a problem: Don't be afraid to send back food that's bad, spoiled, overcooked or undercooked, or which has foreign matter in it. Call the waiter and quietly explain the problem, asking that it be corrected. However, if you find you've ordered a dish that's properly prepared but which you don't like, you should try to eat it (you may find the taste grows on you). If you can't eat it, order something else, but expect to pay for your mistake.

The same is true for wine. After the cork is pulled, it's sometimes given to you for inspection. If it smells of clean wine, the bottle is probably all right. If it smells musty, or if it is dry, the wine may be bad. The waiter will pour a small amount of wine for the person who ordered to taste. If it tastes bad, ask the waiter to taste it. As with food, if the wine is spoiled, send it back without making a fuss. The restaurant can return spoiled wine to the wholesaler, so it loses nothing in bringing you another bottle.

During meals: Some "seconds" are free, but you'll have to pay extra for others. A second cup of coffee is usually "on the house," but some restaurants are beginning to charge for this, as they do for extra tea, milk, and other beverages.

If you're on a meal plan, check out the policy regarding wine or alcoholic beverages—the first drink or glass of wine may be included and you pay for the rest, or you may have to pay for any drinks. Extra bread, butter, jam, or relish are generally included in the overall price. If you aren't sure about the restaurant's policy, ask the waiter.

If you want to relax over extra coffee, cigarettes, or a drink after your meal, be sure there's no one waiting for your table. If you're the last people in the dining room, be considerate of the staff and don't overstay.

The check: Always read the bill carefully and check the addition. If there seems to be an error, ask the waiter to explain—without making a fuss or an accusation. If there's still a problem ask for the maitre d' or manager—again quietly—and accept his or her decision. You can follow up with a letter to the management, if you're still dissatisfied.

Finally, as with everything else on your honeymoon, try to take time to really enjoy what you experience. Take time to smell the roses, taste the wine, and talk. Every enjoyable moment you spend together draws you closer.

14. SOCIAL SKILLS AND CONVERSATIONAL ARTS

GETTING ALONG happily in groups is so important to most of us that there are many, many books on the subject—some concerning shyness, etiquette, and conversation, but all basically talking about dealing with other people. This chapter would be encyclopedic if we tried to cover all points. So we'll just talk about social prospects and problems that involve your honeymoon and your first social experiences as a married couple. If you feel you need more help in getting along with others, by all means explore the self-help books in your library or in bookstores.

You may have taken trips together before, but if you did they weren't like the one you're now planning. This will be the first trip in which you meet people as husband and wife, and it will require some subtle—but important—changes in how you act around other people. Being away from home, you may be meeting types of people you've never met before, perhaps foreigners or celebrities. How do you act with them? You might find yourself feeling unexpectedly shy about being on your honeymoon. And what if you commit a real error, such as accidentally insulting or embarrassing another person in front of others, or causing a minor accident?

All of this is not quite etiquette, although it verges on it. It's more the art of being socially at ease and making those around you feel comfortable being with you.

Meeting People as a Couple

Some couples feel embarrassed about being identified as honeymooners. Being married still seems "unnatural." Perhaps they aren't sure how to act anymore, now that marriage has changed the context of their actions. Small things, like consulting one another about the choice of movies, or holding hands in a restaurant, have a slightly different meaning now that you're husband and wife. Even if you can't quite figure out what's happened, you feel that something is different, and you're right.

Other things change even more radically. Whereas when you were single you could make a date with a friend and just *go,* now your time belongs to *both* of you, and you're expected to consult your mate.

When you meet people now, you aren't meeting them as John Brown and Joan Doe, but as "the Browns," John and Joan. And if this new couplehood is fulfilling and intimate, it can sometimes also be uncomfortable and threatening. Now your mate's social mistakes are not just his or hers—they belong to both of you. You can reflect credit upon one another—but also share the blame.

Maybe we shouldn't feel this way; after all, our new wife or husband is still an individual, responsible for her or his achievements and failures. But nonetheless, we often do. So besides making a good impression yourself, you'll want to help your mate do the same.

You'll need to treat your spouse with respect, in private and around others. This doesn't mean being overly polite and proper; it means treating him or her courteously. In conversations with other people, make sure he or she can join in the discussion, or look for a chance to change the subject so that your spouse can take part.

One young wife still fumes a little, remembering an aspect of her husband's behavior that almost ruined the honeymoon:

"Before we were married, when we were alone together we talked about us, and when we were with friends, we talked about people we knew and what was going on in town, mostly, so it was okay. That's why I was so surprised and upset when we were on our honeymoon and meeting new people for the first time. The first time it happened, Louis and I were sitting by the pool and I started a conversation with this guy by asking him what kind of camera he was using. He told us, and then the next thing I knew, Louis had got the conversation onto football. *I* don't know anything about football, and this guy didn't seem that interested, but he went along with it. I sat there, totally out of it, for almost an hour, finding out more than I ever in my whole life wanted to know about football statistics. . . .

"The same thing happened over and over. Every time we met somebody new—and we're both friendly, so that happened a lot—Louis'd get the conversation onto the three things he was happy talking about—football, the navy, and the fishing in Missouri, which is where we come from.

"The real pits came at a time when we were with another couple in the nightclub at the hotel, talking about the hotel and whether the swimming pool was better or the lake—just being friendly, having a good time. Then Louis got this guy to admit he was in the army. He wouldn't stop talking about the difference between the army and navy and how the navy's better in every way. The band came on with a singer, and he kept on talking. When the band finished, this other couple and I would've loved to talk about something else, but Louis kept us all on the same subject. I wanted to *kill* him.

"Later, when we talked about the problem, Louis realized that he was comfortable talking about only three things—football, the navy, and fishing. Since I had only about three things I could talk about, too, we agreed to try learning about some more things. Also, Louis decided to work at learning to keep his mouth shut and letting other people talk."

How do you start a conversation, and what should you talk about? The first step, naturally, is to introduce yourselves. "Hi, I'm Bonnie Sullivan and this is my husband, John," is simple and straightforward. *Never* refer to your spouse as "the little woman," "my old man," or "the wife."

You can always begin the conversation by commenting on your honeymoon location (you don't have to tell anyone you're newlyweds unless you want to, although sometimes people will guess) and asking why the other people decided on that location. If you're in a honeymoon resort, you can talk about your wedding, courtship, what you'll do when you return home. Ask some of the other couples if anything unusual or amusing happened during their wedding or engagement—or share an anecdote about yourselves. Almost every honeymoon couple has some funny little story to relate.

If another couple are having an argument, don't take sides: no matter what you say, you'll probably be wrong! It's all right, and often necessary, to laugh at the absurdity of life—but never at other people.

One gregarious man who's basically shy when meeting new people just listens for a while before entering the conversation. He and many others agree that a good listener is sometimes the best conversationalist of all!

Since you know you'll be meeting new people, you may want to think a bit about what you can discuss—music, movies, sports, jobs, things about your hometown or state, books, television programs—you'll probably have a long list of topics within a few minutes. If you have special knowledge of an unusual field, other people may be interested in learning about that. Some little-known facts about astronomy or wildlife, for instance, could spark a whole evening's conversation.

Stick with subjects you know something about, and use examples from your own experience. If you're unfamiliar with a topic, ask a question—just because you don't know about everything doesn't mean you're stupid. We can all learn about *something*. Besides, most people are flattered when others are interested in what they're saying, and are eager to explain things on which they're "experts." On the other hand, if you're discussing one of your "pet" topics, don't treat those who aren't familiar with it as though they were idiots.

Do you find that your statements during a conversation often aren't responded to? It could be that you're wording them in such a way that the other person isn't encouraged to give an opinion or express a thought. "There is no such thing as life on other planets," said in a firm tone of voice, pretty much brings *that* conversation to a close, whereas "I don't believe there is life on other planets, but I know a lot of people would disagree— what do *you* think?" not only opens up the conversation but virtually assures at least a minimal response.

If it's obvious that the other person isn't interested in discussing UFOs and such, you can try another subject. Move to something else, but don't make it a huge leap. Go from UFOs to, say, the future of space flight, or a popular movie concerning either of those subjects. If you've tried two or three subjects and the conversation is still sinking, give it up, at least for now. The other person may not feel like talking to you—or anyone—at the moment.

Conversation Killers

Some people have a terrible knack for bringing friendships to an end before they've really begun. And yet just a little thought would tell them that there are some subjects which people react to strongly and which cause disagreements and bad feelings. It's touchy enough if the person who brings up the subject, say, communism as a political system, does so because he or she really wants to hear other people's opinions. But often the person who brings up such a subject does so with the intention of proving to the unfortunate listener that his or her own opinion is the only correct one: "Communism is the only viable system left!" or "The communist menace will bring ruin to us all!"

You're on your *honeymoon*. This is a time to relax, avoid controversy, and have a pleasant time meeting people. This is not a debating event, and even when you win an argument about a controversial subject (and you rarely do—the reason they're controversial is that people have strong opinions about them), you've destroyed the happy, relaxed, and romantic mood that is what a honeymoon is all about.

Another way not to make friends is with racist, sexist, or other "-ist" jokes, even if they're really funny and you think the people you're telling them to can't possibly be offended. At the very least they might find your humor to be in poor taste. And you can't tell for sure who could be offended. That fellow you're victimizing with the joke about the dumb Samoan and the coconut may not be a native of Samoa, but he might have a soft spot in his heart for Samoa or for coconuts.

Breaking the Ice

You're shy, out of your depth, or know nothing about the subject being discussed—now what?

Even the most self-assured people occasionally encounter a person or situation that leaves them feeling shy and awkward. The famous, the rich, the beautiful, aren't exempt, and neither are you. Some people who seem aloof or cold are actually shy and will warm up if given the opportunity. If this is your problem, start combating it by forcing yourself to smile and say "hello" to people. If someone begins a conversation with you, try to give a full answer and, if possible, end with a question that'll keep the conversation going. Don't answer with "yes," "no," "not long," "uh-huh," or other such monosyllabic responses.

If no one approaches you, choose the most friendly and outgoing person in the room and start up a conversation. You might do this by commenting on his or her social skills. "Hi, my name is Joan Levitz and this is my husband, Frank. We couldn't help noticing how at home you seem. Have you stayed here before?" This opens up a multitude of conversational possibilities. You might ask how they like the resort, hotel, or club, have they traveled much, and so on.

Of course, some shy people solve their problem by turning it into an asset—by becoming excellent listeners. This shouldn't be overdone, however, or it becomes phony and irritating.

What if you're not shy, but you really feel out of place? Confess *that*. Say: "I'm really ignorant about anthropology. How did you get involved in it?"

Meeting Foreigners

Whether you meet them in the U.S. or abroad, meeting foreigners is a golden opportunity to learn about other countries and different ways of thinking. If you meet someone from another country who is traveling in America, remember that he or she is probably just a little worried about fitting in, especially if his or her native language isn't English.

Don't speak louder than usual when talking to a foreign person who's having language difficulties, but do speak more distinctly. Don't bring up a touchy political situation, give a negative opinion of the person's home country, praise the glories of America as compared to "lesser" nations, complain about national habits, or make fun of foreign accents. Talk about the same things you'd talk about to anyone, but be especially polite and conservative about expressing your opinions.

Meeting Celebrities

Should you approach a celebrity and introduce yourself? It depends. Interrupting a meal or an obviously private conversation is always rude and is likely to get you, at best, a polite brush-off. Asking for autographs isn't a good idea, since this puts you in the category of either "fan" or "pest," depending on how the celebrity feels about autograph seekers, and wipes out any hope of a real conversation. If you meet a celebrity when he or she is with another, not famous, person, include that person in your greeting and conversation. Most celebrities have been distressed more than once by having persons dear to them ignored and even physically pushed aside.

Approach the celebrity just as you would anyone else—at the right time and in the correct place. Start a conversation as you would with a non-celebrity. The famous person is first and foremost a *person,* concerned with the same things as the rest of us. Introduce yourself and allow the celebrity to introduce him or herself. Don't say, "I know who you are!" and blurt out a name. You might be wrong, which would embarrass both of you.

Celebrities are under constant pressure to be funny, beautiful, brilliant, or whatever it is they're famous for, all the time. They might be grateful to you if you approach them simply and warmly, as one human being to another. You're not only more likely to have an interesting conversation, but to get to know the real person behind the celebrity mask.

If You Blunder

No matter how careful you are, how well behaved, you're going to make mistakes. How do we know? Because everyone does.

If you cause an accident, break something, or accidentally insult or embarrass someone, apologize once—sincerely—and then shut up. Repeated apologies will only prolong the embarrassment for everyone.

Should you accidentally damage or destroy something belonging to another person, apologize and ask if it can be repaired or replaced. If it can, have it done. If you can't restore the object, look for something comparable and send it to the injured party with a nice note.

An embarrassing remark can be even harder to handle. If you can cover it up, do. For instance, you say, "Most civil-service workers don't even put in a full day's work anymore!" and one of the people you're talking to says, "I'm a civil-service worker." Bluff it out! "Really? It must be aggravating for you to have a few lazy people make you all look bad!" The person may not totally swallow it, but it saves face. When there's absolutely no way to wiggle out, be honest and contrite. "I'm sorry. That was stupid of me."

On the other hand, when someone has insulted your religion or broken your engraved cigarette lighter or spilled whiskey on your shoes—accidentally—help him or her out. Think how awful you'd feel if *you'd* done it, and try to lessen the pain.

There's an old story about an elderly fellow going to call on the new neighbors. "What are the people like around here?" the wife asked. "What were they like where you came from?" he replied. "Oh, they were real friendly and helpful." The man nodded. "You'll find they're the same here." On his way out he ran into the husband, who asked the same question. "What were people like where you came from?" the old man asked again. "It was real dog-eat-dog," the husband said, "the most gossipy, suspicious people you'd ever want to meet." The old man nodded. "You'll find they're the same here," he said.

Look for the best in yourselves and in other people. When things go wrong, forgive. You'll meet a lot more nice people that way.

15. ETIQUETTE

The Public You

Etiquette sometimes seems arbitrary. Actually it's behavior that's evolved over generations from necessity or at least sensible practice—a kind of collective wisdom. The Japanese have perhaps the most elaborate etiquette in the world—maybe because, more than most people, they were forced to live in close proximity. They had to evolve customs that enabled them to get through the day's business without continual annoyance.

The *need* for etiquette is unquestionable, but the exact forms change with time and circumstance. Who decides? Everyone. But some people make a study of the subject and set forth rules. The problem is that social arbiters don't always agree among themselves—nobody ever claimed etiquette was an exact science. Most experts, however, would probably concur with the credo of good manners stated more than a century ago in a manual with the no-nonsense title of *Sensible Etiquette of the Best Society:*

Etiquette is the sovereign ruler of social pleasures; its kingdom comprises not only manners, but the application of manners to events. The observance of its laws avoids confusion and maintains decorum, insuring to each individual due attention and respect. Its whole attention is to maintain the dignity of the individual and the comfort of the community.

The language may be a touch flowery, but the sentiment is as sensible as wool in winter.

We'll assume you're already familiar with the basic rules of good behavior—you don't put your elbows in the soup or describe your operation while your companions are eating chopped liver—and go on to special etiquette for situations that may be unfamiliar to many of us.

If you're going on a honeymoon you'll have to get there. You'll have to travel, and travel has its own codes of proper behavior. That's a good place to begin.

Basically, all modern travel consists of being moved in a metal box of some sort in close quarters with strangers—*awfully* close quarters. Let's examine those metal boxes one at a time.

IN AN AUTOMOBILE

It comes down to this—get there in one piece. If you have a driver's license you've already been exposed to the rules of road etiquette, which are simply rules for staying alive while hurtling over asphalt at high speeds:

· Don't cut off other cars.
· Don't tailgate.
· Don't speed.
· Don't blow your horn, except in an emergency.
· Assume the other drivers are either asleep or maniacs, and act accordingly.

One more observation—if you're the passenger, you have every right to request (politely) that the driver slow down or avoid other dangerous practices. There's always another plane or another table at the restaurant—nothing's worth jeopardizing your life or safety.

ON A PLANE

· Be considerate of the other person or persons in your row—confine your possessions to your own space.
· Leave the washroom mirror, sink, and counter clean.
· Be ready to leave when the seat-belt sign goes off. Don't stand

in the aisle collecting your belongings while the passengers behind you wait impatiently.

ON A TRAIN

- If you're in the Pullman section, decide with the other passengers what time the berths should be made up; then advise the porter.
- If you're in an upper berth, the porter will put up the ladder for you.
- If you're in a compartment, summon the porter when you want the bed made up.
- Don't play your portable radio—at least not loud enough for anybody else to hear. Your idea of pleasant listening may be your neighbor's idea of torture.
- Leave washroom, mirror, sink, and counter clean.
- If you have a compartment, your meals may be served there. Otherwise you'll go to the dining car or snack bar (always take your ticket or stub with you). Wait for the steward to seat you.

ON A BUS

The same rules for planes and trains apply to bus travel, plus one other—don't dawdle at rest stops. Nothing is more inconsiderate than keeping fifty people waiting while you finish your second cup of coffee or rearrange your coiffure.

ON BOARD SHIP

- Address the captain and ship's doctor by their titles; other officers as "Mr." or "Ms."
- The chief steward assigns tables for the voyage; check with him or her soon after the ship departs. If you want to change your seating assignment to join friends you've made during the trip, ask the chief steward's permission. There are usually two sittings for each meal—early and late.

A final bit of advice for maintaining good relations with fellow travelers—don't bore them. If people seem friendly and interested, by all means strike up a pleasant conversation; otherwise, respect their privacy. You're on a honeymoon; someone else may be going to a funeral.

AT HOTELS AND RESORTS

As soon as you reach your honeymoon location, you'll probably want to call or send a telegram to your parents to let them know you arrived safely and to thank them for a beautiful wedding. Other than that, you're entitled to privacy from your family and friends.

Be considerate of the hotel staff. However, we don't recommend imitating one bride who confessed that she carried this too far: "The first morning I jumped up and made the bed and tidied the room so the maid wouldn't think I was sloppy."

Another couple recommends making sure the "Do Not Disturb" sign is out when it should be: "We were making love and the maid walked in—surprise!" When you're ready to have the room cleaned, switch to the "Please Make Up This Room" sign. If you aren't dressed when room service arrives, be sure to put on a robe or other non-transparent garment.

Sometimes your hotel or resort will send you flowers or fruit or arrange some other treat because you're honeymooners. This is its way of saying "thank you for coming" and making you want to come back. It's nice to call the manager to express your appreciation or to drop a note to him or her after you get back home.

When in doubt about how to handle any situation involving others, the "Golden Rule" will guide you. For instance, though service personnel, such as hotel or restaurant attendants, are there to serve you, they're still people and they want to be treated with courtesy. You needn't go out of your way to avoid inconveniencing them, but you'll find that good manners usually result in better service.

When something goes wrong, a firm but polite discussion with the people involved greatly increases the chances of correcting the problem. In fact, the best way to approach a difficulty—let's say your air conditioner doesn't work—is to find out who is in charge of that particular area, and approach him or her with the phrase "I have a problem." Then explain. Sometimes you'll be told the repairs will be made, but they will take time. If you feel that the amount of time is too long, say that you understand the difficulty but you'll have to ask for another room. Don't either grit your teeth and stay quiet, or insult the other person. Would you do *your* best for someone who was obnoxious?

SMOKING

It's polite to ask whether those you're with (including your spouse) mind if you smoke. It's also polite to offer a cigarette to others. If one is offered to you and you don't smoke, a simple "No, thank you" is sufficient. Acting self-righteous or making references to cancer will just make everyone else uncomfortable.

Some other pointers about smoking include:

- Don't blow smoke in another person's face.
- Don't smoke during a meal (between courses is all right as long as no one else is still eating). Remember always to ask permission.
- If you're beginning your meal and the person at the next table is having dessert and a cigar or cigarette, say something like "I'm sorry to disturb you, but we've just begun our meal— would you mind smoking outside after you've finished your meal?" If the other person refuses to stop smoking and it's really unpleasant for you, ask the waiter to speak to him or her or to move you to another table.
- Never put ashes in dishes—ask for an ashtray if none has been provided.
- Don't flick ashes onto the carpet, and avoid cigarette burns on furniture.
- Don't "bum" cigarettes.
- If you're camping, hiking, or otherwise outdoors where sparks might cause a fire, "field-strip" cigarettes before discarding them (this means tearing the paper and scattering the ashes once the cigarette is extinguished).

DRINKING

Getting drunk isn't romantic, and hangovers aren't sexy—so take it easy. Nightclubs and resorts often have drinks with names like "Passion Flower" or "Love Potion"—but the only "passion" or "love" you'll feel the next morning will be for aspirin or an ice bag.

ENTERTAINMENT/RECREATION

If you're considerate of other people and use good sense, you shouldn't have any problems in a nightclub or theater, at a sporting event, or participating in an activity. Still, you might not be entirely sure how to act under certain circumstances, so here are a few hints:

Dancing: Enjoy yourselves but don't put on a show—unless you're in a disco. If you want to request a special song, give a note to the waiter or waitress, who will take it to the band. In a piano bar, you can make your request in person. Sometimes restaurants and nightclubs have a minimum, a cover charge, or a music charge. Check the policy in advance.

Live performances: At the theater, a concert, or a nightclub performance, arriving after the show has started is inconsiderate to others in the audience, as well as to the performers. Sometimes latecomers have to wait until the first break or intermission before being seated. Talking, eating, singing along, or making unnecessary noise during a performance disturbs everyone around you. So does taking pictures with a flash attachment (which can also be dangerous to performers). Some places have notices informing customers that cameras and flashes are forbidden.

Games are for amusement and pleasure. Poor losers or people who take games too seriously spoil the fun of those playing with them. In a casino, kibitzers are definitely unwelcome, and the same is true on the tennis court or a golf course. Don't hang over players. At the crap or roulette table, wait for a seat to become available. Sometimes drinks are free for people who are gambling —check the casino policy in advance.

Sports: Common sense is the basis for etiquette in sports. You don't take dangerous chances, such as pointing a gun—even if you believe it's not loaded—at someone else. If you're boating, watch out for diver's flags, swimmers, and water skiers ("don't make waves!"). When diving, check out the swimmers in the pool before springing off. If you're fishing, don't cast near other people and watch for other lines; if you're fishing on a chartered boat, don't take someone else's assigned place. When biking, go in the direction of traffic and keep an eye out for pedestrians.

In team sports, don't criticize other people's playing skills or create an argument over points—this is supposed to be *fun*, remember? And in team sports, be sure to include those players who make up in enthusiasm what they lack in skill. Last—but not last at all in importance—observe the rules and consider your partner's feelings. You didn't marry her because she was a volleyball champion, and he's still a good man even if he can't dive off the highest diving board over the pool. So encourage, don't criticize.

Radio and TV: Keep the volume down.

The Private You

As important as public behavior is, private behavior is even more so. If you offend a waiter or cab driver it will cause, at most, a temporary unpleasantness. But if you're constantly offensive to your mate, you'll eventually have serious problems, no matter how much you may love one another.

You'll be living in an intimacy that's impossible to understand until you've experienced it, and you'll both have adjustments to make. Eventually, you'll evolve your own highly private etiquette that has absolutely no application outside your own four walls but is nonetheless important. You'll decide matters such as who gets the bathroom when, who takes out the garbage, who buys the newspaper, who deals with the breakfast dishes.

But for now, on your honeymoon, you'll be feeling your way. If one of you is having a good time at the club but the other is exhausted and wants to leave, what do you do? Which partner handles waiters or writes thank-you notes for wedding gifts? If you feel you may have embarrassed your mate in front of others, do you apologize then and there? Or wait until you're alone?

Since you might not have had time to work out a mode of living together, some things may be a bit confusing during the honeymoon. Realize that this is a transition period—a time and space between being unmarried and married to this particular person. Realize that this is not a dream, a fulfillment of your fantasies about what a honeymoon is and what it will bring, but a reality. There will be fun and joy and intimacy, but also awkwardness and possibly some pain. Realize the importance of treating your spouse with the same respect you give to others—or, better yet, with *more* respect.

This means respect for your partner's privacy and space, as well as for his or her feelings. Ask permission before borrowing something that belongs to your mate, before you make a date, or before you commit your money to anything. One of the hardest things to get used to is the fact that now your lives, money, and time belong to each other, as a couple. Whereas once it was okay for you to make a decision based solely on your own wants, needs, and priorities, you now have a partner to consult. To deny your husband or wife this consultation on matters that concern you both (even if it's only a doubles tennis game) is to deny that person respect.

The space you occupy also belongs to both of you. One bride complained that her husband, to whom sports were very important, filled their honeymoon getaway car with golf clubs, tennis rackets, bowling balls, and other sports paraphernalia, without consulting her or talking with her to figure out how much space he could have for his things and how much she could have for hers.

A young husband told a story that shows the opposite side of the coin: "When we loaded the car for the honeymoon I discovered that Sandra had enough luggage to live out of for a year, but, this being before the wedding, I didn't want to have a fight, so I didn't say anything. Then when we got to the hotel, she took over the bathroom. I mean she took over! Her underwear, socks, makeup, hair-dryer, you name it—there was about half a soap dish left for me.

"By the third day I felt like a non-person and I was smolder-
ing with anger. Finally we had a talk. A *long* talk. She'd been
an only child, so she was used to having as much space as she
needed for her stuff, but now there were *two* of us. I have to
admit that once I pointed the problem out to her she did things
to make me feel as though I counted too. She wasn't doing anything on purpose. It's just the way she was used to behaving."

The moral is that this couple were able to recognize a potentially dangerous situation and, through discussion, arrive at a
mutually agreeable solution—an etiquette that fitted their needs.
Discussion is the key, and we can't emphasize it enough. Don't
ever grin and bear it. If something is bothering you, speak about
it as soon as you conveniently can. If you don't, you and your
spouse will both bear the brunt of your hostility.

Notice we said that the discussion should take place when
convenient. This is *not* during dinner with another couple. Exposure of the mate's foibles may seem amusing on TV game
shows—those free refrigerators and trips to Hawaii can soothe a
lot of ruffled feathers. In real life, however, it's an inexcusable
humiliation that often ends with somebody sleeping on the couch.

Everyone has hang-ups, sillinesses, and immature traits, regardless of chronological age. If these seriously interfere with
the functioning of your marriage, thrash them out together or
with a sympathetic referee. Often, though, you can learn to
tolerate these things, perhaps even come to regard them with
amused affection, as part of your loved one's uniqueness. You
can't change another person. If you love him or her, you don't
really want to.

In any case, reserve criticisms and questions for moments of
privacy, and even then, be gentle. Present your problems cau-
tiously and quietly, and if possible, work compliments into the
conversation. You aren't a prosecutor. You're a friend. In the
same vein, avoid any put-down or sarcastic humor toward your
mate. He or she may laugh at the moment, but is almost sure to
be wounded.

Some hassles can be solved very practically. We know one
husband who reads mystery novels in bed at night. They're his
lullaby, his sleeping potion, his panacea. His bedtime half hour

with Agatha Christie or Ellery Queen is his reward, and knowing it's coming enables him to remain calm through the grimmest of workdays.

Naturally, he continued this habit through the honeymoon. For three days his wife (who was a morning person, whereas his normal bedtime was one a.m.) suffered through it. Then, in a moment of insomniac depression, she confessed that she absolutely could *not* sleep with the light on. He tried giving up his mysteries for the next two nights and discovered that without them he couldn't sleep. The solution was a tensor lamp with an intense, but very narrow, focus that illuminated his book and *only* his book, plus a sleep mask for his wife. The simplest way is often the best way. An item as ordinary as a lamp, sleep mask, or earplugs (for diminishing radio or TV sound) can save endless arguing and hurt feelings.

It might be a good idea to inventory your habits before you're married. What did your mother complain about? Your brothers and sisters? What drove your roommate up the wall? Then talk over your odd little habits with your intended (again, we're emphasizing *communication*), and try to arrive at the necessary compromises before the problems occur.

You won't always be in the wrong, and something that you think will be a source of irritation may go entirely unnoticed. But unless you come from a large family or have lived in dormitories, you may find that things you take for granted might be offensive to another. An uncapped toothpaste tube may be beneath notice to a husband, but it could set off his wife's inner alarms. A smoker may not realize how disgusting a cigarette butt floating in leftover coffee is to a nonsmoker.

So far, we've been discussing the negative aspects of private etiquette—how *not* to annoy, inconvenience, and drive crazy. But there is a positive, and hugely rewarding, aspect to it. Ever notice an older couple—a man and woman in their eighties, with decades of married life behind them? They *do* things for each other. They constantly practice simple courtesies—opening doors, fluffing cushions, sending the partner a questioning glance when something unexpected comes up.

With these people, private codes of behavior have evolved

beyond the mechanics of daily hassle-free living into a lovely ritual. They're like dancers engaged in a continuing ballet, re-affirming and confirming their regard, respect, and love with every gesture they make. It's beautiful to watch, and more beautiful still to engage in. It's etiquette raised to its highest form, and one of the splendors of marriage.

16. THE MIRROR OF
YOUR IMAGE

WHEN romance goes out of a marriage, it's hardly ever because of one big reason. Most of the time it's from a wearing away of passion caused by tiny neglects and minor annoyances. One area where these annoyances and neglects can arise is in personal grooming.

Grooming chiefly concerns taking care of the outside of you—skin, hair, teeth—but this doesn't mean it isn't important. A national gossip columnist has said that men complain most about their wives wearing hair curlers and face cream and about their wives' insufficient interest in sex. Women complain that their husbands are inconsiderate about smoking and drinking, and that they come to bed with bad breath and without bathing and then expect passion.

It's really sad when one remembers that these are people who had groomed and clothed and behaved with extreme considera-tion on their wedding day. These same people now may take care with their grooming only before going to work, or when going out or meeting strangers. Because their priorities have shifted—from their spouse to outsiders—they take all the care in the world for others, but have little concern about the impression they make on their husband or wife, the person who can contribute most to their emotional happiness.

Grooming isn't some artificial gimmick concocted by ad agencies in order to sell products: you can be well groomed using just soap, water, and a toothbrush. And it isn't something that you need only when meeting strangers.

Caring for your appearance is a way of acting out respect for your mate. He or she deserves the very best of you, not what's left over after you've taken care of the rest of the world.

Put your mate first. When you do, you'll find yourself doing things a little differently. You might bathe at night instead of in the morning, so that you can go to bed fresh and clean. You can (and should) brush your teeth after every meal, not just before work in the morning. A woman will get a haircut that doesn't require her to walk about the house in a bizarre assortment of hair curlers.

Living in a close relationship with another person requires more, not less, effort and thoughtfulness on your part. When marriages fall apart and someone says, "I've never really understood why," maybe what happened was just the sort of petty neglect we've been talking about. Nothing to scream about, but enough to slowly turn your husband or wife off until he or she completely loses interest in you as a lover. Decide now to make good grooming a habit *before* your honeymoon, and to be as considerate of your mate all the days of your marriage as you were on your wedding day.

As we said, you can be well groomed with just water, soap, and a toothbrush, but there are refinements. For these we refer you to some of the excellent books available for both men and women. You might want to take advantage of these now, while you're preparing for your marriage and honeymoon.

Here are a few tips on basic grooming:

Rub-a-Dub-Dub

People who take showers say that lying about in a bathtub isn't good for you because all your dirt stays there with you. Bath people say that if you bathe frequently there isn't that much dirt, and cite the physical and metaphysical virtues of the bath. Who should shower and who should bathe?

Generally speaking, if you have dry skin you should take a bath. Into this bath pour bath-oil beads, bath oil, or other skin soothers. Bathing two or three times a week is enough, using a washcloth when needed and a footbath now and again in between. During the winter too much bathing may cause dry skin to itch, especially if you haven't been using bath oil. If you do have dry, itchy skin but want to bathe every day, use bath oil and a neutral (pH-balanced) soap. Also great for dry, delicate skin are oatmeal, buttermilk, and cold-cream soaps.

For some people, a nightly bath is more than a method of getting clean. It's a blessed time of privacy, an opportunity to wash away a day's accumulated tension so they can face the evening relaxed and refreshed. One dermatologist says: "A soaking bath is a good way to relax, and on that basis tension is eased; however, a bath and a shower clean the skin equally well."

If you want a more invigorating bath, use tepid, not hot, bath water and either soak in the tub and then shower off, or shower first and then soak. Whichever pattern you follow, you might enjoy using a rough loofah, a stiff hemp mitt, a natural bristle brush, or a sponge (for delicate skin), to rouse your circulation. Your skin will tingle delightfully and glow beautifully afterward.

On the other hand, there's nothing like a shower, especially in the morning, to get you going. Showers are also good for relaxing stiff muscles, although not as good as a bath. Wonderful additions to shower equipment are massaging attachments—adjustable nozzles that create a pulsating stream of water. If you have dry skin, use neutral or superfatted soaps, and stroke on bath oil while your skin is still wet. If your skin is oily, a shower is perfect. Use either a neutral or medicated soap and a loofah, hemp mitt, or natural bristle brush to remove dead layers of skin, which can cause blemishes.

How Nice You Smell!

Women: With so many different types of scents available—bath oil, scented body lotions, powders, soaps, colognes, perfumes—you can always find something to fit your life and your mood.

Things to consider: First of all, your particular body chemistry is going to interact with whatever fragrance you use, to produce a unique effect. Once in a while you might come across a scent that smells just awful on you, even though it was great in the bottle. That's why, when shopping for cologne or perfume, you should take advantage of the bottles offered for testing. Put a little perfume on your wrist or the inside of your elbow, and go on with the rest of your shopping. If it smells good a half hour or so later, then it might be for you.

Perfume lasts much longer than any other kind of scent, but costs a lot more. Only you can decide if the extra cost is worthwhile—just don't forget that a little perfume goes a long way, whereas colognes may have to be splashed on with abandon to get the strength and effect you want. Solid perfumes last longer because they don't evaporate as quickly as liquids. If you use an atomizer it'll disperse cologne better.

When you use scent, apply it to wrists, throat, the crook of elbows, behind your knees. Don't use perfume if you're going to spend time in the sun. You could have an allergic reaction and/or experience splotchy discoloration.

Men: While you men will be applying a light scent with your after-shave balm, don't stop there. Use a complementary cologne, applying this to your neck and chest, where it'll last longer. If you have dry skin, the fragrance won't last as long as on normal or oily skin. On the other hand, oily skin can change a cologne's characteristics dramatically. To try a cologne, rub a little on the back of your hand. Don't smell it immediately. The release of alcohol disguises the true, more lasting scent. After several minutes, sniff and decide.

Finishing Touches

Hands: They move, they touch, and by their texture and appearance, they tell a lot about you. When you touch your mate, how do you want your hands to feel? Some men do work that leaves their hands rough and stained so that even the gentlest caress feels like sandpaper on tender skin, and some women grow nails so long that they look like glass claws. The man needn't give up his job, nor the woman her choice in how she looks, but he or she can make small concessions for the mate's comfort. If you do any sort of work that makes your hands rough, use hand lotions regularly. File your nails smoothly and keep them short enough so they won't accidentally scratch. If you can, use protective gloves for any job that will stain or roughen your skin.

Hair: What's good for your hair is good for you—good diet, cleanliness, healthy circulation. In fact, if your hair is limp, dull, and generally blah, take a look at the rest of you. A major change in your diet and life-style (and maybe even a checkup with your doctor) may be in order. It's okay to wash your hair daily, provided you use a shampoo that's mild enough for your type of hair. When shampooing, be sure to rinse thoroughly, since left-in shampoo dulls the hair. Try testing different brands to find the right one or ones for you. Changing your shampoo from time to time also helps spark up your hair.

When choosing a hairstyle, you should consider what kind of impression you want to make, your type of hair, and how much "fussing" will have to be done with it. Consider the pros and cons of coloring, highlighting, or streaking your hair. Remember that electric curlers, blow dryers, and curling irons are a boon if you don't want to wear curlers to bed or for any length of time. Above all, be sure to get a good cut and keep it trimmed.

Makeup: Experiment to find a look that's appealing and that conveys the real you. Take advantage of the makeup counters at department stores, but don't be a slave to their advice. Ask for samples so you can experiment at home. If your skin is oily, water-based cosmetics are best, whereas if your skin is dry, oil-based ones are good. Your basic makeup "wardrobe" could consist of a foundation, face powder, blusher, eye shadow, eye liner, mascara, and lipstick. If you feel adventurous, there are plenty of other products to choose from. Regardless of your selections, there is one basic rule: always apply your makeup to a clean face.

People differ on the merits of sleeping with makeup on. Some say "never," while others say it's okay as long as you clean your face gently and carefully at least twice a day. Try a few nights of washing your face, reapplying your makeup, and sleeping with it on. Then see how your husband *and* your skin react before forming your own opinion.

Your skin has several enemies, with the sun leading the list. So when sunbathing, use a sunscreen with PABA on the label. Tan slowly; limit yourself to fifteen minutes the first few days. Don't think you're protected just because you're under an umbrella, in the water, or wearing a hat. Both sand and water reflect the sun.

You should also remember when sunning that the hours from 10 to 2 are roughest on the skin and that you can get burned on a cloudy day or in winter. Continue using a lotion even after you've acquired a tan. Be sure to use extra protection on eyelids, knees, and other spots not normally exposed to the sun. If you're at a high altitude, you'll need even more protection because there's less atmosphere to absorb the sun's rays.

If you're taking medication, be sure to talk with your doctor; some medicines make skin more sensitive to the sun.

Smoking is another great enemy. Wrinkles and discoloration occur with constant exposure to burning tobacco. Excessive drinking of alcohol leads to dry skin. Stress and facial grimaces are also bad for your skin.

On the other hand, your skin's benefactors include a balanced diet, fresh air, a happy outlook, physical exercise, regular sleep, and a lack of tension. So smile and relax. Every now and then, treat yourself: splurge on a day of facials, pedicures, manicures, leg waxing, and makeup lessons.

Remember: all great things are made up of a multitude of

small things. Good grooming done for love of your mate will be one of those small things that contributes daily to a happy marriage.

17. THE STAY-SEXY
DIET

ROMANTICS who want to stay sexy and healthy would be better off if the proverbial "a jug of wine, a loaf of bread, and thou" had been written "a glass of wine, a single roll, and thou." The poem might have been less exotic, but the calories would be fewer. Anyway, too much wine is not only fattening, but is notorious for interfering with sexual performance.

A sexy body is a healthy one; and a healthy body is one that's not lugging around a lot of extra fat. So if you're overweight or gaining unwanted or unneeded weight—a frequent problem for engaged couples under the stress of planning their wedding and honeymoon and enjoying parties celebrating their engagement— this section is for you.

Several insurance companies publish height-weight charts which you can use as a guide to your correct weight—just don't kid yourself that you have a "large frame" when you really are small- or medium-boned. You also can do a skinfold test. This involves pinching an area of skin between your thumb and forefinger and measuring the distance between the two. About half of our total body fat is deposited under the skin, so if you can pinch a skinfold more than one inch thick (men) or one and one-half inches thick (women) on your abdomen under the navel, you are overfat.

Permanent weight loss requires a change in eating habits and an increase in physical activity. These two acts, more than any crash diet, will produce the desired results and help you maintain that new figure once you achieve it.

Diet

Nutritionists and other health specialists recommend a gradual weight loss of one or two pounds per week if you want to achieve long-term results. Fad diets for quick weight loss are often followed by regaining the lost weight once you return to your former eating habits. By going more slowly and learning to modify your eating habits as you go, you're less likely to experience a relapse.

The best diet is one that includes a variety of foods for nutritional balance. No one category of foods is "fattening" per se. For good health, our bodies need the nutrients in protein and dairy foods, carbohydrates (fruits, vegetables, and grains), and fats each day. What is fattening is excessive quantities of any of these. Here are guidelines for a balanced diet recommended by many nutrition authorities:

Protein Foods: Two or more servings per day, up to 12 percent of your total caloric intake. A serving is three ounces of cooked fish, poultry, or meat; one egg; and two tablespoons peanut butter.

Dairy Products: Two or more servings per day. These should be counted as part of the total protein percentage of your daily calories. A serving is eight ounces of milk, plain yogurt, or cottage cheese; and one ounce of cheese.

Fruits/Vegetables: Four or more servings per day. A serving is one-half cup or a medium-size fruit or vegetable. These should include a good source of vitamin C (citrus fruits, berries, tomatoes, dark green vegetables) and a good source of vitamin A (dark green and deep yellow vegetables) each day.

Starchy Foods: Four servings per day. These and the fruits/vegetables servings together should equal 58 percent of your total caloric intake. A serving is one slice of bread; one-half cup rice, pasta, or legumes; a small potato; and one roll, muffin, pancake, or waffle.

Fats/Oils: Two tablespoons per day maximum. In combination with fats in meat, poultry, fish, dairy products, and some vegetables, these should equal 30 percent of your total caloric intake.

The above guidelines apply whether you want to take off excess pounds or just maintain your present weight. If weight loss is your goal, these additional suggestions may help:

1. Select lower calorie foods in each of the above categories. To compare the calories and nutritional value of similar foods, read the nutrition labels found on many processed foods. You also may want to invest in a paperback copy of a calorie-counter book.
2. Use skim-milk dairy products, which are lower in calories and fat content than whole-milk products.
3. Fish, poultry, and veal are generally lower in calories and fat content than red meats.
4. Eat more egg whites and fewer yolks (yolks contain all the fat and most of the calories; the whites are pure protein).
5. Eat polyunsaturated fats (from vegetable oils) rather than saturated fats (from animal sources, coconut, or palm oil), whenever possible.
6. Trim excess fat from meat and remove skin from poultry (where fat is concentrated) before cooking.
7. Prepare foods by dry broiling (without butter or oil) or steaming to preserve more nutrients and eliminate calories from added fats. Also, using cookware with a premium non-stick coating reduces the need for added oils when cooking.
8. Fats take longer to digest than carbohydrates or proteins, so a meal that has a high fat content makes you feel fuller for a longer time after you've finished. And if you feel fuller, you're less apt to feel energetic and ready for action—of any sort.
9. Select foods packed in water rather than oil; in natural juices rather than syrups.
10. Eliminate or greatly reduce your intake of sugar and products made with sugar, much of which is "hidden" in processed foods such as canned and frozen fruits, canned vegetables, soups, breads, ready-to-eat cereals, frozen meals and snacks,

sauces and salad dressings, and fruit drinks and yogurt. Sugar goes by many names, including caramel, syrup, honey, molasses, natural sweeteners, and anything ending with "-ose" in a list of ingredients. All add non-nutrient calories.

11. Eat more fruits, vegetables, and whole grain foods.

12. Eliminate or greatly reduce your intake of salt. Again, read the labels on foods for "hidden" salt content.

13. Salt-free bouillon or consommé, tomato juice, or a large salad makes a good first course and helps curb the appetite.

14. Don't keep high-calorie snacks or "danger" foods (anything you just can't resist overeating) in the house.

15. Stock up on low-calorie substitutes for those times when you have the "munchies." Raw fresh vegetables and fruits are satisfying and nutritious, too. So are dried fruits, but don't overdo —the calories in these can quickly add up to an excess.

16. Eliminate or greatly reduce your intake of sauces, gravies, and salad dressings, all of which tend to be calorie-laden. Use spices to liven up low-calorie mayonnaise, plain yogurt, or low-fat cottage cheese for a salad dressing substitute. Or try using seasonings and a few squeezes of fresh lemon juice instead of dressing—this also will perk up many vegetable dishes and fish, poultry, and meats.

17. Eliminate or reduce your intake of alcoholic beverages, which are high in calories. They may be used in cooking to enhance flavors, however, since most of the calories are burned off when alcohol is heated.

18. Serve smaller portions and use smaller plates to make them appear larger.

19. Eat slowly, so your stomach has time to tell your mind that you're full (this takes about thirty minutes). Try putting down your utensils between each bite.

20. Set small goals for yourself. Aim for a series of losses of two pounds each instead of one gigantic loss of fifteen pounds. And reward yourself when you reach each goal with a small non-food treat such as a record album or book you've been wanting, a new scarf or jogging outfit, flowers, tickets for a movie or concert. This—and the way you look and feel as the pounds diminish—will encourage you to continue.

Exercise

Exercise goes hand in hand with a good diet for weight loss or maintenance, since the number of calories you consume versus the number you expend produce the end result.

In addition to burning up calories, regular exercise offers the additional benefits of improved body tone, increased energy, and better overall fitness. Good brisk walking is one of the best and easiest forms of exercise, especially for beginners. Jogging, bicycling, roller or ice skating, swimming, tennis, racquetball, and rope-jumping are also popular ways to keep in shape. The trick is to choose some type of vigorous exercise that you'll enjoy and then to stick with it. Once a week on the tennis courts simply isn't sufficient for good health.

If you haven't exercised for a while, you'll want to begin slowly and gradually increase the amount of time and energy you put into your exercise program. The result of too much, too soon, is often pulled or strained muscles, which certainly isn't an incentive to continuing—so easy does it!

In addition to a planned program of exercise, there are all sorts of ways to sneak in a little exercise throughout the day— walking up and down stairs instead of taking the elevator, getting off the bus several blocks before your stop and walking the extra distance, doing a few deep knee bends or stretches while you talk on the telephone. You probably can think of others that will fit into your life-style.

Lightweight Recipes for Lovers

To get you going on your weight-loss program, here are some recipes using aphrodisiacs (see Chapter 13) and our diet tips. Each is designed to serve two.

EGGS ITALIANO

1 large firm tomato, halved
2 tablespoons fresh bread
  crumbs
2 tablespoons shredded
  mozzarella cheese
1½ teaspoon chopped parsley

½ teaspoon basil
Pepper, to taste
2 eggs
1½ teaspoon diet margarine,
  melted

Preheat toaster oven to 425° F. Scoop out pulp and seeds from tomatoes; reserve for soup or sauce. Place each tomato shell, cut side up, in an individual casserole dish sprayed with non-stick spray, and bake for 5 minutes. Meanwhile, combine crumbs, cheese, parsley, basil, and pepper. Break one egg into each tomato shell; top with crumb mixture. Drizzle with melted margarine. Bake until eggs are set and topping is golden (about 10 minutes). About 160 calories each.

NEPTUNE'S DELIGHT

2 fresh fillets of sole
1 cup dry white wine
½ cup water

1 teaspoon lemon juice
Herbed Avocado Sauce (see
  below)

Roll fillets and secure with toothpicks. Heat wine, water, and lemon juice to a boil in 2-quart saucepan. Reduce heat and place rolled fillets in liquid. Poach, covered, over low heat for 5 minutes. Remove with slotted spoon and chill fillets, if desired. Serve with Herbed Avocado Sauce. About 160 calories each.

HERBED AVOCADO SAUCE

1 soft California avocado,
  peeled and seeded
1 egg yolk
1 tablespoon tarragon vinegar
1 tablespoon lemon juice
½ teaspoon Dijon mustard

1 teaspoon dried or fresh dill
  weed
1 teaspoon fresh parsley,
  chopped
Pepper to taste

Combine ingredients in blender and blend until smooth.

MYSTIC MUSHROOM AND SNOW PEAS

3 ounces snow peas (Chinese pea pods)
½ cup sliced mushrooms
2 tablespoons soy sauce

2 teaspoons minced fresh ginger root
1 garlic clove, crushed

Steam snow peas and mushrooms until just tender. Drain off any excess liquid. Heat skillet with premium non-stick finish over medium heat. Transfer vegetables to skillet; add soy sauce, ginger, and garlic. Stir until liquid is almost completely evaporated. About 30 calories per serving.

CHICKEN HISAE

12 ounces skinned and boned chicken breast, cut into 1½-inch pieces
1 tablespoon soy sauce

1 tablespoon rice vinegar
1 tablespoon chicken bouillon
1 garlic clove, crushed
1 ounce scallions, chopped

Heat skillet with premium non-stick finish over medium heat. Add chicken pieces. Brown on one side; turn and brown on other side. Add soy sauce, vinegar, bouillon, and garlic. Cover; cook for 2 minutes. Remove cover; turning pieces occasionally, allow liquid to reduce completely. Sprinkle with scallions before serving. About 200 calories per serving.

EVE'S GARDEN

¼ cup unsweetened pineapple juice
¼ cup apple juice
¼ cantaloupe, scooped into mellon balls
1 sweet red plum, quartered

and sliced into chunks
3 slices unsweetened canned pineapple, quartered
15 Thompson seedless grapes
2 tablespoons low-fat yogurt (*optional*)

Add fruit juices to a skillet with premium non-stick finish; cook over medium heat until mixture begins to bubble. Stir in fruits;

continue simmering until most of the liquid has been reduced. Mixture will be somewhat thick. Remove from heat and cool to room temperature. Serve in sherbet glasses with a spoonful of low-fat plain yogurt, if desired. About 75 calories per serving.

TROPICAL STEAKS

2 4-ounce minute steaks
1 beef bouillon cube
¼ cup water
½ teaspoon cornstarch
¼ teaspoon basil, crumbled
Pepper to taste

1 small garlic clove, crushed
1 medium firm banana, peeled and quartered
1 small tomato, cut into 8 wedges
¼ cup sliced onion

Trim any fat from edges of meat. Combine bouillon cube, water, cornstarch, basil, pepper and garlic. Heat skillet with premium non-stick finish; brown steaks quickly on both sides. Remove to serving platter and keep warm. Add remaining ingredients to skillet and heat to boiling. Simmer 3 to 4 minutes, until hot and cooked. Return steaks to skillet and heat to serving temperature. About 295 calories per serving.

AFTERWORD

WE get from life what we give to it.

If we expect that life will be dull or filled with constant strife, we approach it as an adversary rather than as an exciting opportunity to enjoy and test ourselves. But if we approach life with love and enthusiasm, it repays us in the same coin.

It's the same way with marriage. If we expect that once the honeymoon is over we'll settle down into a dull domesticity, we're unlikely to make efforts to explore the many rich and enjoyable aspects that this truly remarkable relationship can yield. For what is marriage? It's two people who trust each other enough, in an untrusting world, to go together into an unknown future; who love enough to let their mate come closer to them than anyone has been before.

Life and marriage can't always be exciting and fulfilling, but they can be richer than we sometimes think. We have only to make an effort.

So think of yourselves as perpetually on your honeymoon. Take care to attract your mate and to please your mate. Keep your honeymoon savings account alive by making small but regular deposits, and try to get away, if only for a weekend, every three to six months—for a honeymoon, not a vacation! Make time to relax and concentrate on one another, to renew the affection and commitment between you.

Your honeymoon need never end.

After the Honeymoon Is Over

We'd like to hear from you. Tell us about your experiences—good or bad—with the resources listed in THE HONEYMOON

HANDBOOK. Do you have any comments, suggestions, additions, or corrections you think we should make in the next edition? Do you have any honeymoon experiences you'd like to share with us? This form, like the entire book, is for you to use any way you like.

- -

Name_____

Address_____

Comments, Complaints, Suggestions, Experiences to Share_____

_____

_____

_____

_____

_____

_____

Send to:

Romantic Travelers, Inc.
151 East 50th St.
New York, NY 10022

- -

Section Five

NUTS AND BOLTS

---

18. INTRODUCTION TO SECTION FIVE

WHAT FOLLOWS is, in many ways, the nuts and bolts of this handbook. Here we provide you with numerous resources that enable you to follow up our suggestions in the preceding text and that make your lives easier. While we have striven to be comprehensive, it would have been impossible to list every possible resource. Under books, for instance, we have merely given you a sampling of what's available.

We have included as many addresses as possible. Although we have tried to be up-to-date, it is almost a truism that any guide of this nature is outdated the moment it is published. Frequently we listed the address of an organization's national headquarters. You should check your local telephone book—both white and yellow pages—for local affiliates before writing the national office. Also check your local phone book for the proper way to place toll-free calls.

We suggest that whenever writing for booklets, you inquire as to any charge and send a stamped self-addressed envelope along with your request.

When we mention that a place publishes certain booklets or we suggest that you ask for a particular publication, this does not mean that that is the limit of materials available.

Try to be as specific as possible whenever making an inquiry. While specificity does not guarantee a complete answer tailored to your needs, it does increase the possibility.

TOLL-FREE NUMBERS

These frequently vary from area code to area code. Your best bet is to check first with the Toll-Free Information Operator at

800-555-1212. In addition, there are directories of toll-free numbers. You might want to look for these on the reference shelves
at your local library.

Finally, we cannot guarantee that you will receive answers
from every place to which you write or that the answers you do
receive will be up-to-date or thorough. Allow yourselves plenty
of time. Nor do we vouch for the quality of any organization,
service, or publication listed. If you run into a problem, be sure
to complain—we give you lots of information about how to do
just that—and let us know by completing the form at the end
of Section Four.

HAPPY HONEYMOONING!

Schedule for Planning a Honeymoon

As Soon as Possible

1. Talk about the kind of honeymoon you want.
2. Begin your research. Collect magazine and newspaper articles, visit the library, talk to friends and relatives.
3. Determine the budget for your honeymoon.
4. Call or write hotels, tourist bureaus, resorts, airlines, other
   carriers for brochures.
5. Consult a travel agent.
6. Begin planning and budgeting trousseau.

Four to Six Months Ahead of Time

1. Make transportation and lodging reservations, including a
   state or national park if this is your honeymoon choice.
2. Find out what immunization shots you might need. Some immunizations require a series of shots spaced out over a period
   of time. You also should allow time to recover from any side
   effects.
3. Apply for a passport and any visas you'll need if traveling
   abroad.
4. Visit a gynecologist, especially if you are already having sex-

ual relations and haven't consulted a gynecologist yet. Check about rubella immunization.

Three Weeks Ahead of Time

1. Reconfirm hotel reservations in writing.

Ten Days Ahead of Time

1. You should receive your tickets, hotel confirmations, other materials from your travel agent.

Seventy-two Hours in Advance

1. Reconfirm an international flight.

Twenty-four Hours in Advance

1. Reconfirm a domestic flight.

Immediately After the Ceremony; Before Leaving

1. Sign the marriage certificate; arrange for its safekeeping while you're away.

Immediately Upon Arrival

1. Call your families with the news of your safe arrival.

The Day After

1. Send a thank-you telegram to the bride's parents thanking them for the wedding and reception.

19. A DIRECTORY OF ROMANTIC TRAVEL POSSIBILITIES:

General Resources

Bride's magazines
Friends, relatives
Lecture programs offered by churches, museums, universities
Libraries
Speakers' bureaus run by airlines, other travel-industry organizations
Travel magazines
Travel section of your local newspaper

BOOKS/BOOKLETS

Numerous guidebooks are published annually. Among the most helpful are those produced by Temple Fielding, Eugene Fodor, Arthur Frommer, Robert S. Kane, Myra Waldo, and Michelin. Check the most recent copyright date for an indication of when the guidebook was last revised. You might also want to check:

The Adventurer's Guide by Jack Wheeler (McKay, 1976)
Business Week Diary and Business Travel Planner by Business Week Staff (McGraw-Hill, 1976)
Fair Weather Travel in Western Europe by Edward D. Powers (Mason & Lipscomb)
Going My Way: A Travel Editor's Guide to Getting More for

Less by Carolyn and Charles Planck (Celestial Arts Publishing). For the leisurely traveler.

How to Travel Without Being Rich by Norman D. Ford (Harian Publications)

Information Please Almanac special section on travel (Viking Press, 1978)

Let's Go: Europe put out by Harvard Student Agencies (Dutton, 1980)

Mort's Guide to Low-cost Vacations & Lodgings on College Campuses (CMG Publishing Co., 1101 State Rd., Princeton, NJ 08540). International and U.S. and Canada editions.

1977 National Directory of Free Tourist Attractions edited by Raymond Carlson (Pilot Books, 347 Fifth Ave., New York, NY 10016)

1001 Sources for Free Travel Information by Jens Jurgen (Travel Information Bureau, P.O. Box 105, Kings Park, NY 11754)

Passport Budget Guide (Passport Publications, Box 24684, Los Angeles, CA 90024)

Selected Guide to Travel Books by Susan Nueckel (Fleet, 1974)

The Travel Catalogue by Karen Cure (Holt Paperback, 1978)

Traveler's Almanac by Bill Muster (Rand McNally)

The World Traveler's Almanac (Rand McNally, 1978)

Consumers' Guide to Federal Publications
U.S. Government Printing Office
Washington, DC 20402

Consumer Information Center
Pueblo, CO 81009

Catalog of government publications, many of which are useful for travelers.

Handbook for Travelers in the U.S.
Meridian House Foundation
1630 Crescent Place, NW
Washington, DC 20009
(Also available in French, Portuguese, Spanish.)

Holiday Travel Newsletter
1100 Waterway Blvd.
Indianapolis, IN 46202

Honeymoon Resorts

There are many such resorts across the country. Some of them are very posh; others are more modest. Consult your travel agent and travel publications for more specific information. You may also contact the following associations:

American Bridal Institute
122 E. 42nd St.
New York, NY 10017

Pocono Mountains Honeymoon Center
Box PR
1004 Main St.
Stroudsburg, PA 18360

OTHER RESOURCES

Very Special Places by Ian Keown (Collier Books, 1978). Mostly expensive resorts.
Very Special Resorts (Berkshire Traveller Press, Stockbridge, MA 01262)

Hotels, Motels, and Inns

BOOKS

America on $8 to $16 a Night—4000 Dining and Lodging Discoveries (Travel Discoveries, 10 Fenway North, Milford, CT 06460, 1977)
Caribbean Hideaways by Ian Keown (Harmony Books)
Classic Country Inns of America: New England and the Maritimes; The Mid-Atlantic and The South; and The Pacific

Coast and the Southwest (3 vols.) edited by Peter Andrews (Holt, Rinehart & Winston, 1978)

Country Inns and Back Roads by Norman Simpson (Berkshire Traveller Press, Box G, Stockbridge, MA 01262)

Country Inns of the Far West by Rachel Bard, Jacqueline Killeen, Charles Miller, and Peter and Neva Vogel (101 Productions, 834 Mission St., San Francisco, CA 94103)

Country Inns of Maryland, Virginia and West Virginia by Lewis Perdue (Washingtonian Books, 1828 L St., NW, Washington, DC 20036)

Gomer's Budget Travel Directory (Hammond, Inc., Maplewood, NJ 07040, 1979)

Historic Country Inns of California by Jim Crain (Chronicle Books, 870 Market St., San Francisco, CA 94102, 1977)

The Inn Book: A Field Guide to Inns & Good Food in New York, New Jersey, Eastern Pennsylvania, Delaware and Western Connecticut by Kathleen Neuer (Random House, 1976)

National Directory of Budget Motels by Raymond Carlson (Pilot Books, 347 Fifth Ave., New York, NY 10016)

The 1980 Complete Directory of the Leading Hotels of the World (Hotel Representatives Inc., 770 Lexington Ave., New York, NY 10021)

Very Special Places by Ian Keown (Collier Books, 1978)

Where to Stay USA (Council on International Educational Exchange(777 United Nations Plaza, New York, NY 10017)

BOOKLETS/OTHER PUBLICATIONS

Passport to Inexpensive European Hotels
Voyager, Ltd.
Box 24684
Los Angeles, CA 90024

Sav-on-Hotels
Travel Tips
P.O. Box 1061
Oakland, CA 94611
(Described as a "MiniGuide to 600 Tested Budget Hotels Plus 750 Selected Motels Across Europe.")

U.S. Travel Service
14th and Constitution Ave., NW
Washington, DC 20230
(A list of historic or landmark country inns.)

American Youth Hostels
National Campus
Delaplane, VA 22025
(Listing of hostels throughout the United States and in other countries.)

Lodging with a Difference

CAMPS FOR ADULTS

Club Getaway
951 Second Ave.
New York, NY 10022
212–935–0222

Camp Carefree
2920 Upton St., NW
Washington, DC 20008
212–799–5896
202–362–6525

DUDE RANCHES

Dude Ranchers Association
2822 Third Ave. N.
Billings, MT 59101

Colorado Dude and Guest Ranch Association
Box 6440
Cherry Creek Station
Denver, CO 80206

The state tourist bureaus of Arizona, Nebraska, New Mexico, New York, Oregon, and Wyoming.

FARM VACATIONS

Farm and Ranch Vacations, Inc.
36 E. 57th St.
New York, NY 10022
(Publishes *Country Vacations U.S.A.;* Pat Dickerman, editor.)

Special Reports Division
Office of Communication—Room 460A
U.S. Department of Agriculture
Washington, DC 20250
(Lists state agricultural and travel information agencies that can provide names of guest ranches and farms in their states.)

National tourist bureaus can provide information about arranging farm vacations in foreign countries.

HOUSEBOATING

Contact the local Chamber of Commerce or Tourist Bureau.

Bridge Bay Resort
10300 Bridge Bay Road
Redding, CA 96001

Buck Creek Dock
Lake Cumberland
Rte. 7
Somerset, KY 42501

Bullfrog Marina
Hanksville, UT 84734

Canyon Tours
Box 1597
Page, AZ 86040

Captain Sunshine
RR 3
Box 294K
DeLand, FL 32720

Grider Hill Dock
Lake Cumberland
Rte. 4
Albany, KY 42602

Holiday Harber
Box 112
O'Brien, CA 96070

Lake Mohave Resort and Landing
Bullhead City, AZ 86430

Lazy Days Houseboats
Box 819
Bethel Island, CA 94511

Lee's Ford Dock
Lake Cumberland
Box 753
Somerset, KY 42501

Link's Landing Inc.
Osage Beach, MO 65065

London Boat Dock
Lake Cumberland
Rte. 1
London, KY 40741

New Hope Landing
Box 417
Thorton, CA 95686

Northernaire Floating Lodges
Box 510
Island View Route
International Falls, MN 56649

Riverdale Resort
Rte. 1, Box 56
Buchanan, TN 38222

Ron's Houseboat Rentals, Inc.
Box 1122
Tavernier, FL 33070

S&H Boat Yard
Box 514
Antioch, CA 94509

Trillium Charters
11 Graham Ave.
St. Catherines, Ontario, Canada

Van's Motor Marine, Inc.
5 Sisson St.
Alexandria Bay, NY 13607

INDIAN RESERVATIONS

American Indian Travel Commission
10403 W. Colfax Ave.
Lakewood, CO 80215
(The commission can also give you information on Indian events.)

ROUGHING IT

In a cabin in a U.S. forest:

Supervisor
North Unit
Tongass National Forest
Box 1049
Juneau, AK 99801

National Forest Recreation Association
22841-A Media Lane
Cupertino, CA 95014

National Park Concessioners
1003 Abby Way
McLean, VA 22101

Also:
Outward Bound
165 Putnam Ave.
Greenwich, CT 06830
(Survival training.)

TOURS

Questers Tours and Travel
257 Park Ave. S.
New York, NY 10010

Travcoa
875 N. Michigan Ave.
Chicago, IL 60611

1900 Ave. of the Stars
Los Angeles, CA 90067

Society Expeditions
P.O. Box 5088
University Station
Seattle, WA 98105

South American Wilderness Adventures
1769-NS Solano Ave.
Berkeley, CA 94707

TREKS

Some of these require plenty of time, as well as good physical condition and a sense of adventure.

Earth Explorer
1560 Sandburg Terrace
Chicago, IL 60610

Earthwatch
P.O. Box 127 PG
Belmont, MA 02178
(Scientific expeditions.)

Exodus Expeditions
167 Earls Court Rd.
London SWF 9RF, England

Mountain Travel
1398 Solano Ave.
Albany, CA 94706

Trail Finders Ltd.
48 Earls Court Rd.
London SWF 9RF, England
(Publishes *The Trail Finder*.)

WAGON-TRAIN TREKS

Bar-T-Five Outfitters
Jackson, WY 83001

The Dakota Wagon Train
Eagle Butte, SD 57625

Honeymoon Trail, Inc.
Moccasin, AZ 86022

Wagons Ho
Main Street
Quinter, KS 67752

L. D. Frome
Wagons West
Afton, WY 83110

Wagons West
Western Travel Merchants
P.O. Box 1570
Cody, WY 82414

ZEN RETREATS, MEDITATION CENTERS

A Pilgrim's Guide to Planet Earth (1979). Travel guide plus
listings of gurus, hospitals, spiritual centers throughout the
world.

The Spiritual Community Guide (1977). Lists yoga and medita-
tion centers, natural food stores and restaurants, spiritual
retreats.
The New Consciousness Source Book (1979)
(All from The Spiritual Community, P.O. Box 1080, San Rafael,
CA 94902)

The California Bosatsukai Flower Sangha
5632 Green Oak Dr.
Los Angeles, CA 90028

San Francisco Zen Center
300 Page St.
San Francisco, CA 94102

Zen Studies Society
223 E. 67th St.
New York, NY 10021

Zen Mountain Center
Tassajara Springs
Carmel Valley, CA 93924
(A retreat to visit.)

Special-Interest Ideas

GENERAL

Explorer's Ltd. Source Book by Explorer's Ltd. (Harper & Row,
1977)
Worldwide Tour Guide (Official Airline Guide, 1980). Ask your
travel agent to let you look through the "Special Interest
Tours" section.

AMUSEMENT PARKS

The Great American Amusement Parks by Gary Kyriazi (Citadel
Press, 120 Enterprise Ave., Secaucus, NJ 07094, 1976)
Directory of Amusement Parks (International Association of

Amusement Parks and Attractions, 7222 W. Cermak Rd., N. Riverside, IL 60546)

BICYCLING

Associations

American Youth Hostel Association
National Campus
Delaplane, VA 22025

American Wheelmen
Box 988
Baltimore, MD 21203

Bikecentennial
P.O. Box 8308
Missoula, MT 59807
(A 4,450-mile Transamerica Bicycle Trail. There are smaller trails scattered across the country.)

International Bicycle Touring Society
2115 Paseo Dorado
La Jolla, CA 92037

Books/Booklets

The Best of Bicycling edited by Harley M. Leete (Trident Press, 1972)
Bicycling and Bicycle Trails (National Technical Information Service, 5285 Port Royal Rd., Springfield, VA 22151). A bibliography.
The Complete Book of Bicycling by Eugene A. Sloane (Trident Press)
How to Improve Your Cycling (Bicycle Institute of America and Amateur Bicycle League of America, Athletic Institute, Chicago, IL 60606)
New York Bicycler by Rafael Macia (Fireside—Simon and Schuster)
North American Bicycle Atlas (American Youth Hostels, 20 W. 17th St., New York, NY 10011)

Other Countries

National tourist boards and airlines can tell you more about bicycling abroad.

BIRD WATCHING

Nature Guide
34915 4th Ave. South
Federal Way, WA 98002
(A listing of people across the country who will give the traveling bird watcher or nature lover information about their area.)

The Audubon Society
950 Third Ave.
New York, NY 10022
(List of phone numbers to dial for news of local bird spottings.)

BLUEGRASS

Bluegrass Unlimited Magazine
Box 111
Broad Run, VA 22014
(Puts out a free list of bluegrass festivals annually.)

CAMPING / BACKPACKING / HIKING / OUTDOOR RECREATION

Booklets

Camping With Ease, Backpacking With Ease, and *Traveling With Ease* (The Dow Chemical Company, Consumer Products Dept., P.O. Box 68511, Indianapolis, IN 46268)
Outdoor Safety Tips and *Visit a Lesser-used Park* (Supt. of Documents, U.S. Government Printing Office, Washington, DC 20402)

These and other government publications are also available from U.S. Government bookstores in major cities. Check your phone book for one near you.

Professional Tips on Keeping Warm and Dry (Royal Red Ball, Dept. GO, P.O. Box 1148, Elkhart, IN 46514)

The U.S. Travel Service (14th and Constitution, NW, Washington, DC 20230) has special brochures on different sections of the country and on specific national parks. Other U.S. Travel Service brochures include *Travel a New World of the Great Outdoors* and *National Parks, Their Purposes and Management.*

Many national tourist boards in other countries publish camping guides. Also, many national foreign airlines have fly-and-camp package arrangements—ask.

Books

Adventure Travel North America (Adventure Guides, 36 E. 57th St., New York, NY 10022)

The All Outdoors Cookbook by William B. McMorris (McKay, 1974)

The Backpacker's Budget Food Book by Fred Powledge (McKay, 1977)

Backpacking and Outdoor Guide by Richard Dunlop (Rand McNally, 1979)

The Camper's Cookbook by Ruth L. Schubert (Little, Brown & Co., 1974)

Campgrounds and Trailer Parks Guides (Rand McNally, 1978)

The Complete Book of Mountain Sports by Curtis W. Casewit (Messner, Julian/Simon & Schuster, 1978)

Cooking Over Wood by Phillip Jones (Sterling, 1976)

Country New England Recreation and Sports Guide by Anthony Hitchcock and Jean Lindgren (Burt Franklin/Lenox Hill, 1978)

Europa Camping and Caravaning Directory edited by Dier Schmoll (Europa, 2306 Sixth St., Clay Center, KS 67432, 1978)

The Great Outdoors Guide by Val Landi (Bantam, 1978)

Index to Outdoor Sports, Games and Activities by Pearl Turner (Faxon, 1978)

National Park Guide by Michael Frome (Rand McNally, 1980)

Off and Walking by Ruth Rudner (Holt, Rinehart & Winston, 1977)

1,001 Tips for the Great Outdoors by Walt Leonard (Contemporary Books, 1978)

Outdoor Recreation in America by Clayne R. Jensen (Burgess, 1977)

The Outdoors Survival Manual (Sterling, 1978)

Recreational Vehicles Campground and Service Directory (Trailer Life, 1980)

Simple Foods for the Pack by Vikki Kinmont and Claudia Axcell (Sierra Club Books, 530 Bush St., San Francisco, CA 94108, 1976)

Stalking the Faraway Places by Euell Gibbons (McKay, 1973)

Walking Tours of America by Kinney Shoe Corp. and Wayne Barrett (Macmillan, 1979)

Wilderness Canoeing & Camping by Cliff Jacobson (E.P. Dutton)

Campgrounds—National/State Parks

National Forest Service
U.S. Department of Agriculture
Washington, DC 20250

National Park Service
U.S. Department of the Interior
19th and E Streets, NW
Washington, DC 20240

U.S. Army Corps of Engineers
Washington, DC 20314

When writing the Army Corps of Engineers, ask about their Camp-a-Float Cruiser program. This allows you either to bring your own recreational vehicle and rent a cruiser to take you on federal waters, or to rent a cruiser complete with recreational vehicle.

U.S. Bureau of Outdoor Recreation
Box 7763
Washington, DC 20004

Directory of all federal recreation centers; includes information on admission fees and on the Golden Eagle Pass.

For information about state parks, write the Department of Parks, c/o State Capitol, in the capital of the respective states. Space in many New York and Virginia state parks can be reserved through Ticketron offices.

Private Campgrounds/Recreational Facilities

American Forest Institute
1619 Massachusetts Ave., NW
Washington, DC 20036

Family Camping Federation
Bradford Woods
Martinsville, IN 46151
(Information on renting house trailers, mobile homes, and recreation vans, as well as on campsites.)

Holiday Inn Trav-L Parks
3796 Lamar Ave.
Memphis, TN 38118

Kampgrounds of America, Inc.
Mutual Benefit Life Bldg.
Billings, MT 59103
(Offers a rent-a-tent program at two hundred U.S. and Canadian campgrounds.)

Other Resources

County Extension Service agents

Local chambers of commerce

Organizations

American Youth Hostels Association
National Campus
Delaplane, VA 22025

Appalachian Trail Conference
Box 236
Harpers Ferry, WV 25425

1718 N St., NW
Washington, DC 20036

Fédération Française de Camping & Caravaning
78 Rue de Rivoli
Paris, France

Kinney Walking Tours
P.O. Box 5006
New York, NY 10022
(Prepares tour packets for the West, South/Southwest, Midwest, and East. Also provides packets on jogging trails from coast to coast.)

Sierra Club
530 Bush St.
San Francisco, CA 94108

Wilderness Society
729 15th St., NW
Washington, DC 20005

Wilderness Southeast
Rte. 3, Box 619
Savannah, GA 31406

CANOEING

American Canoe Association
4200 E. Evan Ave.
Denver, CO 80219

Books/Publications

Adventure Travel (Adventure Guides, Inc., 36 E. 57th St., New York, NY 10022, 1980). Contains a comprehensive list of canoe areas and outfitters.

Introduction to Water Trails in America by Robert Colwell (Stackpole Books, Cameron and Kelker Streets, Harrisburg, PA 17105)

Wilderness Canoeing by John W. Malo (Macmillan, 1972)

FESTIVALS

Festivals and other special events of all types are held annually throughout the U.S. and in foreign countries. The subject might be antique airplanes, cherry blossoms, wildfowl carving, Amish pageantry, arts and crafts, or any one of dozens of other possibilities. When writing to a state or national tourist bureau, be sure to inquire about any special events that might be scheduled for the time of your visit.

The National Association of Travel Organizations (1100 Connecticut Ave., NW, Washington, DC 20036) publicizes the top twenty travel events for each month throughout the country. Check your local newspapers for this information.

FISHING

"Fishing in Kentucky"
Kentucky Department of Fish and Wildlife
Capital Plaza Tower
Frankfort, KY 40601

Louisiana Department of Tourism
Department of Culture, Recreation & Tourism
P.O. Box 44291
Baton Rouge, LA 70804
(Provides a list of charter boats for Gulf fishing.)

Orvis Vermont Fly-Fishing School
10 River Rd.
Manchester, VT 05254
(Three-day course in fly-fishing; cost includes lodging and meals.)

FOLK ARTS

National Council for the Traditional Arts, Inc.
1357 Connecticut Ave., NW
Suite 1118
Washington, DC 20036
(Puts out a directory that lists gospel-singing events, fiddling contests, and Indian, ethnic, and other events.)

GOLF

Robert F. Warner, Inc.
630 Fifth Ave.
New York, NY 10020
(This is a hotel representative specializing in golf resorts throughout the United States.)

HISTORIC PLACES

AAA, Fodor, and Mobil have guides to historic houses.

An American Heritage Guide to Historic Houses of America (American Heritage Publications)
America's Historic Houses: The Living Past (Country Beautiful, Waukesha, WI 53186, 1967)
American Travelers' Treasury: A Guide to the Nation's Heirlooms by Suzanne Lord (William Morrow, 1977)
Discover Historic America by Robert B. Konikow (Rand McNally)
Great American Mansions and Their Stories by Merrill Folsom (Hastings House, 10 E. 40th St., New York, NY 10016, 1976)
More Great American Mansions and Their Stories by Merrill Folsom (Hastings House, 10 E. 40th St., New York, NY 10016, 1979)
National Register of Historic Places (Supt. of Documents, U.S. Government Printing Office, Washington, DC 20402)

HORSEBACK RIDING

American Forestry Association
Dept. A
1319 18th St., NW
Washington, DC 20036
(Provides brochure of scenic trails.)

Adventure Travel by Pat Dickerman (Adventure Guides, Inc., 36 E. 57th St., New York, NY 10022, 1978)
Farm, Ranch and Country Vacations by Pat Dickerman (Adventure Guides, Inc., 36 E. 57th St., New York, NY 10022, 1979)
Horseback Vacation Guide (Stephen Greene Press, Brattleboro, VT 05301)

HOT-AIR BALLOONING

The Balloon Federation of America
Suite 430
821 15th St., NW
Washington, DC 20005
(For names of balloonists in the area you plan to visit or for special events scheduled.)

NUDE BATHING (otherwise known as clothing-optional beaches)

Publications

Dare to Go Bare
American Sunbathing Association
810 N. Mills Ave.
Orlando, FL 32803
(A directory of camps.)

Free Beaches
P.O. Box 132
Oshkosh, WI 54901
(A guide to nude beaches and swimming places in the U.S. and Canada.)

Nude Resorts and Beaches
Popular Library
600 Third Ave.
New York, NY 10016

The Natural Life . . . *the Family Nudist Magazine*
1134 Haverhills Rd.
W. Palm Beach, FL 33409

Nude Life Magazine
Box 296
Indian Springs, NV 89018

Tours

VIB
444 Madison Ave.
New York, NY 10017
(The initials stand for Vacations in the Buff.)

Skinny Dip Tours
30 E. 42nd St.
New York, NY 10017

SAILING

Annapolis Sailing School
Box 1669
Annapolis, MD 21404
(Offers a cruising vacation with instruction; also operates out of
Key Largo and St. Petersburg, Florida.)

Offshore Sailing School Ltd.
820 Second Ave.
New York, NY 10017

Check the Yellow Pages or the classified ads in *Sail* magazine
for other sailing schools. You might also want to read *Royce's
Sailing Illustrated* by Patrick Royce (Japan Publications).

SCUBA DIVING

If you want to learn this sport before heading off on an island honeymoon, check the Yellow Pages under "Divers" and "Skin Diving Instruction." Many local YMCAs also offer lessons.

The Divers Training Academy
R.F.D. 1
Box 193-C
Ft. Pierce, FL 33450

SHAKESPEARE

Shakespeare Association of America
61 Broadway
New York, NY 10016
(For a schedule of Shakespeare festivals.)

SKIING

The Breckenridge Ski Schools
Box 1058
Breckenridge, CO 80424

National Ski Areas Association
61 S. Main St.
West Hartford, CT 06106

Ski the High Sierra Association
P.O. Box 2007
Olympic Valley, CA 95730

Ski the Rockies News Bureau
Suite 1500
666 Fifth Ave.
New York, NY 10019

Ski Tourist Council, Inc.
342 Madison Ave.
New York, NY 10017

Ski Touring Council
Troy, VT 05868
(Publishes *The Ski Touring Guide,* a list of ski-touring or cross-country skiing centers across the United States.)

Student Ski Association
223 N. Pleasant St.
Amherst, MA 01002

U.S. Ski Association
Suite 300
1726 Champa St.
Denver, CO 80202

Winter Recreation Safety Guide
U.S. Government Printing Office
Washington, DC 20402
(Booklet on ski safety and ski touring, with maps and information about winter safety and survival.)

S P A S

The Health Spas by Raye and Robert Yaller (Woodbridge Press, 1975)
Secrets from Super Spas by Emily Wilkens (Grosset & Dunlap, 1977). Lists spas around the world.

S P E L U N K I N G

Wolfcreek Wilderness
P.O. Box 596
Blairsville, GA 30512
(Information on weekend expeditions; cost includes lodging and food.)

S P O R T S   G E N E R A L L Y

See your local bookstores or libraries for innumerable how-to books on individual sports. You might be interested in the following:

A Carnival of Sports: Spectacles, Stunts, Crazes and Unusual Sports Events by William Severn (McKay, 1974)

Country New England Recreation and Sports Guide by Anthony Hitchcock (Burt Franklin, 1978)

Thrill Sports Catalogue by Consumer Guide Editors (Dutton, 1977)

S W I M M I N G

Book Dept.
International Swimming Hall of Fame
1 Hall of Fame Dr.
Fort Lauderdale, FL 33316
(Provides a complete list of books and pamphlets on the sport.)

Chairman
AAU Masters Swimming
115 Pantry Rd.
Sudbury, MA 01776
(For information about different swimming programs throughout the country.)

Swim Master Newsletter
2308 N.E. 19th Ave.
Fort Lauderdale, FL 33305

T E N N I S

The Tennis Catalogue by Moira Duggan (Macmillan)

W I L D L I F E   T O U R S   A N D / O R   C A M P S

National Audubon Society
Harwinton, CT 06790

National Wildlife Federation
1412 Sixteenth St., NW
Washington, DC 20036

New York Zoological Society
Animal Kingdom Tours
P.O. Box 108
Bronx, NY 10460

Sierra Club
530 Bush St.
San Francisco, CA 94108

W I N E

There are vineyards in Maryland, Michigan, and Oregon as well as the better-known ones in California and New York. In all, more than twenty states have vineyards. Many vineyards sponsor tours and/or have tasting rooms that are open to the public. You should check in advance for the days and hours. Some guidebooks and other sources of information are:

Adventures in the Wine Country by Jefferson Morgan (Chronicle Books, 870 Market St., San Francisco, CA 94102). About northern California.

California's Wine Wonderland
Wine Institute
165 Post St.
San Francisco, CA 94108

Wine Country: California (Sunset Books, Lane Publishing, Menlo Park, CA 94025, 1977)
Wine Country USA/Canada (Raymont Associates, 1975)
A Wine Tour of France by Frederick Wildman (Morrow, 1972)

Wine World Magazine
15101 Keswick St.
Van Nuys, CA 91405

Winery Tours of Oregon, Washington, Idaho and British Columbia by Tom Stockley (The Writing Works, 7438 S.E. 40th St., Mercer Island, WA 98040, 1978)

Champagne News and Information Bureau
522 Fifth Ave.
New York, NY 10036
(Champagne region of France.)

Napa County Development Council
P.O. Box 876
Napa, CA 94558
(Provides a map with the vital information on the back.)

Wine Tours International
Box 2536
Napa, CA 94558

Winegrowers Council of Oregon
816 S.W. First Ave.
Portland, OR 97204

T R A V E L   C L U B S

Airline Passengers Association
P.O. Box 2758
Dallas, TX 75221
800–527–6006
(One benefit of membership is a toll-free number that connects
you with Oceanographic Services forecasters who can supply a
two- or three-day forecast for any major city in the world.)

The Chalet Club
135 E. 55th St.
New York, NY 10022

Club d'Azur
200 Park Ave.
New York, NY 10017
(For seafarers.)

Club Internationale
1707 L St., NW
Washington, DC 20036

Club Med, Inc.
40 W. 57th St.
New York, NY 10019

9841 Airport Blvd.
Los Angeles, CA 90045

2 Place Ville Marie
Suite 459
Montreal, P.Q., Canada H3B 2C9

Club Universe
Unitours Bldg.
6171 Wilshire Blvd.
Los Angeles, CA 90017

International Leisure Club, Ltd.
400 Madison Ave.
New York, NY 10017

Matterhorn Sports Club
3 W. 57th St.
New York, NY 10019
(Not limited to sports activities.)

Smithsonian Associates Travel Program
A & I 1270B
Smithsonian Institution
Washington, DC 20560

United European American Club
500 Fifth Ave.
Suite 1821–22
New York, NY 10036
(Transportation only.)

Also check out:

Your alumni associations
Museums
Professional organizations

20. HOW TO WRITE
BUSINESS LETTERS THAT
GET RESULTS

ANY TIME you write for information or to make a reservation or a complaint, you're writing a business letter. To make sure your letters do their job of getting the response you want, follow these suggestions:

- Always repeat important information in every letter. Even if you write to a company or organization many times, repeat the details: *who* you are and *where* you live, *when* you expect to arrive, *what* services you are purchasing at *what* price, *what* services you believe to be included for that price.
- If you have a health problem, be sure to mention it in every letter you write so that the persons involved can make any special arrangements that are necessary.
- Be sure to mention you'll be honeymooning in case the company offers special extras or services for honeymooners.
- Either type or write neatly. If possible, use good-quality stationery, preferably of a plain businesslike design.
- If all's gone well at your honeymoon hotel or resort, write a letter to the management thanking them for a wonderful stay and mentioning any staff members who were particularly helpful and courteous.
- If you must write a letter of complaint, be sure to point out those features and service people who made your stay more enjoyable than it might have been. Not only is this simply fair: it's more likely to result in action. Your complaints will seem more valid when considered next to your willingness to give credit where it's due.

- When making a complaint, be courteous. The person who receives your complaint may not be (and probably isn't) directly responsible for your bad experience. If the person to whom you're writing *is* responsible, he or she will respond best to polite but firm complaints.
- If you can, suggest what sort of action would make the situation better. For instance, if you paid for a room with air conditioning and it didn't work all (or part of) the time you were there, ask the management to make a partial refund as a compensation for your discomfort.
- If the place against which you have a complaint is part of a chain and your complaint is serious, look up the name of the president, manager, or vice-president in charge of operations—*not* the chairman of the board—and write a letter to him or her. You can find the name of the top person to contact with the help of your local librarian or by calling the company and asking for the person's name.
- You might want to send your letter of complaint by registered mail so that you can prove the letter was received.
- If your first letter of complaint goes unanswered, write another one and mention at the end that you're sending a copy of your original letter of complaint to the state and local Better Business Bureaus and Chambers of Commerce. Then do just that. If the complaint is so serious that the matter seems close to fraud, mention also that you're sending a copy of the letter(s) to the state attorney general and the county district attorney—and do that as well.
- For a serious complaint, you might want to end your letter with the warning that you are willing to pursue the matter until you've received some sort of satisfaction.
- Be sure to use the same name in all correspondence in order to avoid confusion.

The following sample letters are intended to serve as a basic guide to the sort of letters you might write when making arrangements for your honeymoon accommodations. We've made up a resort and a mythical couple—you should adapt the letters, therefore, to your own real-life circumstances. On every letter you write be sure to include in the upper right corner your address and the date. In the left corner, just above the body of the letter, include the address of the place to which you're writing.

> 1222 American Lane
> Morristown, Wisconsin
> Zip code
> Date

Mr. Felix Bridwell
Amazing Travel Inc.
Delirium, Wisconsin
Zip code

Dear Mr. Bridwell:

My fiancée and I are planning a honeymoon for the week beginning May 1.

Our ideal honeymoon location would be one at which we could enjoy a wide variety of outdoor sports as well as moderately luxurious accommodations and a sophisticated night life.

We are primarily interested in the Midwest or South, and our budget is approximately $_____$ for up to _____ days.

If you think you could meet our requirements within our budget, we would be interested in hearing from you about potential plans. One final consideration is that June, my fiancée, must observe a salt-free diet.

We look forward to hearing from you soon.

Sincerely,
John Jones

> 1222 American Lane
> Morristown, Wisconsin
> Zip code
> Date

ABCland National Tourist Bureau
123 Street
Big City, New York
Zip code

Good Morning:

My fiancée and I plan to honeymoon in ABCland for the first two weeks of May. We are quite excited about the prospect of visiting your country, and we have several questions:

Will it be possible for us to stay in a castle? Or on a farm?

What are the restrictions, if any, on bringing currency into your country?

What restrictions are there on bringing a camera and film into the country?

What immunization shots will we need?

Do we need any documents other than our U.S. passports?

Where can we purchase a pass for your national railroad system?

We would like to spend some time bicycling around your country-side. Therefore, could you please tell us how to go about renting bicycles, and where we can obtain information about bicycle trails.

Finally, we both love classical music, and are curious to learn whether any symphony concerts are scheduled for the time we'll be visiting ABCland.

Thank you for your attention to our request. We look forward to receiving your reply.

Sincerely,
John Jones

1222 American Lane
Morristown, Wisconsin
Zip code
Date

Manager
Happy Honeymoon Hotel
333 Landfield Blvd.
Rapture, Illinois
Zip code

Good Morning!

My fiancée and I plan to honeymoon for one week beginning May 1 and are interested in staying at your hotel.

Please send us complete information on rates, including those for any package plans you may have; available recreations and activities; and any interesting attractions in the area. Is a car necessary to get around, or is there good public transportation?

We would appreciate receiving this information as soon as possible. Thank you.

Sincerely,
John Jones

1222 American Lane
Morristown, Wisconsin
Zip code
Date

Rapture Chamber of Commerce
Main Street
Rapture, Illinois
Zip code

Good Morning!

My fiancée and I are interested in staying at the Happy Honeymoon Hotel for one week beginning May 1. We would appreciate receiving any information you could supply as to complaints you may have received about the Happy Honeymoon Hotel in the last year or so.

In addition, please send us information on the various tourist attractions in the area. We are also interested in learning of any special events that might be scheduled for that week.

Thank you for your assistance.

Sincerely,
John Jones

(You can also send an inquiry of this sort to the local Better Business Bureau.)

1222 American Lane
Morristown, Wisconsin
Zip code
Date

Ms. Amelia Brown, Manager
Happy Honeymoon Hotel
333 Landfield Blvd.
Rapture, Illinois
Zip code

Dear Ms. Brown:

Thank you for the information you sent on your hotel.

We have decided to spend our honeymoon with you and would appreciate your making a reservation in the name of June and John Jones for one week, beginning May 1. We would like the bridal suite, if that is available, or the next best quality room if not.

We are pleased that your hotel offers the special rate of $_____ for this accommodation and that the rate includes use of all the facilities as well as a daily champagne breakfast in bed. We would like to have fresh flowers and champagne in our room upon our arrival at approximately 7 P.M. on May 1, and would be grateful if you could make sure this is done.

We would also appreciate your informing the chef that June Jones will require a salt-free diet.

Enclosed is a check for $_____, as requested, to serve as a deposit.

Please confirm this reservation as soon as possible.

Sincerely,
John Jones

(To be mailed approximately three weeks before honeymoon.)

1222 American Lane
Morristown, Wisconsin
Zip code
Date

Ms. Amelia Brown, Manager
Happy Honeymoon Hotel
333 Landfield Blvd.
Rapture, Illinois
Zip code

Dear Ms. Brown:

This letter is to reconfirm our reservation for the bridal suite for the week beginning May 1. As per our agreement, the $_____ all-inclusive fee entitles us to the use of all facilities as well as a daily champagne breakfast in bed.

We also wish to thank you for agreeing to have fresh flowers and champagne in our room for our 7 P.M. arrival.

Sincerely,
John Jones

1222 American Lane
Morristown, Wisconsin
Zip code
Date

Reservations
Pegasus Airlines
Morristown, Wisconsin
Zip code

Good Morning!

I am writing to request written confirmation of my reservations for two first-class seats aboard Pegasus flight 653 leaving from Morristown, Wisconsin, at 5:30 P.M. on May 1 and arriving in Rapture, Illinois, at approximately 6:20 P.M. of the same day.

Please advise me by return mail when and where I may pick up my tickets.

Sincerely,
John Jones

(If you have dietary or other special requirements you would state them at this point, in writing.)

1222 American Lane
Morristown, Wisconsin
Zip code
Date

Ms. Amelia Brown, Manager
Happy Honeymoon Hotel
333 Landfield Blvd.
Rapture, Illinois
Zip code

Dear Ms. Brown:

We are writing to tell you how much we enjoyed our honeymoon at your hotel. The staff—especially Mr. Williams at the front desk—were helpful and friendly, and the service was a pleasure. We will certainly be glad to recommend the Happy Honeymoon Hotel to our friends.

Sincerely,
John and June Jones

1222 American Lane
Morristown, Wisconsin
Zip code
Date

Ms. Amelia Brown, Manager
Happy Honeymoon Hotel
333 Landfield Blvd.
Rapture, Illinois
Zip code

Dear Ms. Brown:

We regret to inform you that the quality of accommodations and the level of service offered to us at your hotel were much lower than we were led to expect by both your brochure and your personal assurances.

The tennis and riding facilities were too limited for the number of people who wished to use them, so that we had to stand in line for a half hour or more; service in the dining room was so slow that our food was often cold before it reached us; and our air conditioner in the bridal suite did not work the entire time we were there.

While the inconvenience caused by the wait for facilities and the slow dining room service will just have to be chalked up as experience, we do feel that we paid for the deluxe suite *with* air conditioning, not without. Although you stated that you could not make a partial refund when we last talked, we hope you will reconsider. We would gladly accept any reasonable amount.

Since we feel very strongly about this matter, we are willing to pursue it until we are given some satisfaction.

Sincerely,
John and June Jones

P.S. One of the brighter aspects of our stay was the fine service offered by Mr. Williams at the front desk.

Copies to:
Illinois Chamber of Commerce/Illinois Better Business Bureau
Rapture County Chamber of Commerce/Rapture County Better Business Bureau
Amazing Travel Inc.

1222 American Lane
Morristown, Wisconsin
Zip code
Date

Mr. Felix Bridwell
Amazing Travel Inc.
Delirium, Wisconsin
Zip code

Dear Mr. Bridwell:

We're sorry that we have to write to tell you that our stay at the Happy Honeymoon Hotel was a terrible disappointment. As you can see from the enclosed copy of our letter to Ms. Brown, the facilities were overcrowded, the dining-room service was slow, and our air conditioner didn't work the entire time we were there. Although we complained about the air conditioner the first day and asked to be moved, we were told that the hotel was full and they couldn't transfer us. We also found out that because of a convention in Rapture the other hotels were also full.

We have asked Ms. Brown to suggest a partial refund, which she has so far been unwilling to do. Perhaps she would be more responsive to you. In the meantime, we don't feel that we—or you—should in all conscience recommend the Happy Honeymoon Hotel to others.

Sincerely,
John and June Jones

Business and Consumer Affairs Resources

The following are good places for lodging complaints, checking out businesses and products, and learning how to be a wise consumer:

Consumer Federation of America
State and Local Organizing Project
1012 14th St., NW
Washington, DC 20005
(Directory of local consumer groups. $2)

Council of Better Business Bureaus
National Headquarters
1150 17th St., NW
Washington, DC 20036

Council of Better Business Bureaus
National Advertising Division
845 Third Ave.
New York, NY 10022
(For complaints about national advertising claims.)

Food and Drug Administration
Dept. of Health, Education and Welfare
Public Health Service
5600 Fishers Lane
Rockville, MD 20857
(Publishes *Consumer's Guide to the FDA.*)

Office of Consumer Affairs
Dept. of Health, Education and Welfare
621 Reporters Bldg.
Washington, DC 20201

Call for Action
1785 Massachusetts Ave., NW
Washington, DC 20036

Consumer Affairs Division
Office of the Ombudsman
Department of Commerce
14th and E Streets, NW
Washington, DC 20230

Consumer Information Center
Dept. 623E
Pueblo, CO 81009

Credit Union National Association, Inc.
Box 431B
Madison, WI 53701
(Publishes *Complaints Directory for Consumers.* $1.25)

Federal Trade Commission
Office of Public Information
6th Street and Pennsylvania Ave., NW
Washington, DC 20580

National Consumers League
1028 Connecticut Ave., NW
Washington, DC 20036

Consumer Guide to Product Information
Box 607
Tenafly, NJ 07670
(Published by Bristol-Myers.)

Consumer Resource Guide
Dept. 532G
Consumer Information Center
Pueblo, CO 81009
(Lists federal, state, local agencies; Federal Information Center phone lines; tips on getting action.)

The Help Book: A Guide for Your Survival, by J. L. Barkas (Charles Scribner's Sons)

21. ABOUT GETTING THERE

Air Travel

Major airlines, both national and foreign, are sources of many package deals. Frequently these combine flying with other modes of transportation such as cruise ships, automobiles, and campers. Or they are designed around a special interest. The airlines can also be the source of rail passes, museum passes, coupons for gasoline, and so forth. Don't be bashful. State your interests and needs as precisely as possible. Airlines are listed in the Yellow Pages of the telephone book. Address your inquiries to the Tour Department.

If you require a special diet or are disabled, be sure to inform the airline or your travel agent well in advance so that proper arrangements can be made.

BOOKLETS

Air Travelers' Fly-Rights
Bureau of Consumer Protection
Civil Aeronautics Board
1825 Connecticut Ave., NW
Washington, DC 20428

All About Baggage
You and Your Ticket
Travel for the Handicapped
Director of Consumer Affairs
United Airlines
P.O. Box 66100
Chicago, IL 60666

American Airlines Pocket Seating Guide
P.O. Box 3730
New York, NY 10017

Consumer Guide to International Air Travel
Civil Aeronautics Board
Washington, DC 20428

Consumer Product Information
Pueblo, CO 81009

Facts and Advice for Airline Passengers
Aviation Consumer Action Project
Box 19029
Washington, DC 20036

Pocket Flight Guide
Official Airline Guide
OAG Publications
Reuben H. Donnelley Corp.
2000 Clearwater Dr.
Oak Brook, IL 60521

CHARTER FLIGHTS

See also "Travel Clubs" in Chapter 21.

Association of American Air Travel Clubs
Box 245
Bellvue, WA 98009

Travel Information Bureau
P.O. Box 105
Kings Park, NY 11754
(Request information on the book *How to Fly for Less* by Jens
Jurgen; enclose self-addressed stamped envelope.)

Charter Flights
Office of Consumer Affairs
Civil Aeronautics Board
Washington, DC 20048

Council on International Educational Exchange
205 E. 42nd Street
New York, NY 10017

236 N. Santa Cruz Ave.
Los Gatos, CA 95030

Good Deals
1116 Summer St.
Stamford, CT 06905
(Newsletter.)

Travel Smart
Communications House
Dobbs Ferry, NY 10522
(Monthly newsletter.)

Jax Fax (Jet Airtransport Exchange)
(Ask your travel agent if you can look at a copy of this monthly publication, which gives information on charter fares.)

COMPLAINTS

Bureau of Consumer Protection
Civil Aeronautics Board
1825 Connecticut Ave., NW
Washington, DC 20428
(Twenty-four-hour telephone service: 202–382–7735.)

The CAB has field offices in a number of cities to handle complaints. These cities are Des Plaines, Illinois; Fort Worth, Texas; Los Angeles; Miami; New York; and Seattle.

FEAR OF FLYING

Fearful Flyers
Pan American
30 S. Michigan Ave.
Chicago, IL 60603
(Information on classes to help people overcome this fear.)

GETTING THE MOST FOR YOUR MONEY — SOME GUIDELINES

1. Shop around. Find out all the airlines going to your destination and what discount fares each offers.
2. Consider flying at night or in midweek.
3. Remember that many special fares don't apply over holidays or to and from certain resorts during peak seasons.
4. Use a travel agent to do your leg work for you. But be sure to press him or her to obtain the best possible deal for you. Also keep an eye out for discount flights that are not offered through travel agents, for example, the Laker Skytrain to London.

5. Find out if you can get a lower fare by including your accommodations in your transportation package.
6. Inquire carefully into all restrictions. Many discount fares do not permit stopovers or changes in itinerary without a penalty.
7. Ask about family plans. Ask whether a one-way ticket is less expensive.
8. Pay for your ticket as far in advance as possible. This protects you against fare increases. You're entitled to any fare decreases; be sure to inquire.
9. Invest in trip cancellation insurance if you're going on a charter flight.
10. Consider flying standby or budget.

YOU SHOULD ALSO KNOW ABOUT

Compensation

You may be entitled to compensation if you're bumped off your flight and the carrier can't get you to your destination within certain time limits.

You may also be entitled to compensation if your flight is delayed or cancelled.

You must, however, have conformed to the airlines' regulations regarding check-in, confirmation, and similar procedures.

Lost Tickets

An airline ticket is as good as money, so protect it accordingly. If you lose your ticket, report the loss to the airline immediately. You will need the ticket number, so it is a good idea to note down this number and keep it in a place separate from the ticket itself. If you paid cash for the ticket you will probably have to pay out another full fare in order to be able to go on your trip, since it will take time for your refund application to be processed. If you charged your ticket, you can get a replacement if you are able to produce a record of the charge and proper identification. You must fill out a lost-ticket application supplied by the airline in order to get a credit for the lost ticket.

Quiet Spaces

For long flights, many international carriers block off a quiet zone behind first class. This zone is for passengers who want to work, sleep, or not be disturbed by children, in-flight movies, or lots of attention from flight attendants. You must request this space when making your reservations.

Fuel Surcharges

When purchasing your ticket, be sure to determine whether the price is guaranteed or whether you may have to pay a surcharge imposed later to cover increased fuel costs. On scheduled domestic flights, the airline cannot increase the price once the ticket has been sold. The same, however, is not true for international or charter flights. For these, the airline can increase the price by up to ten per cent; however, passengers will not be allowed to cancel reservations without a penalty.

If You Miss the Plane

The airline will book you on the next *available* flight and honor your tickets. Unless you are on some special fare which has specific restrictions, tickets are good for up to one year from date of purchase (at the time this book went to press).

Insurance You Don't Need

Flight, travel, or any other type of insurance that covers accidental death. If you have properly provided for your beneficiary's or beneficiaries' needs with insurance covering death by natural causes, there is no need for additional coverage. The same is true for double-indemnity riders on life insurance policies.

Automobile

BOOKS / BOOKLETS

Diesel Stop Directory (Hammond, Inc., Maplewood, NJ 07040)

Handbook of Savings for Automobile Owners
Car/Puter
1603 Bushwick Ave.
Brooklyn, NY 11207

How to Deal With Motor Vehicle Emergencies
U.S. Dept. of Transportation
National Highway Traffic Safety Administration
Office of Distribution
Room 4423
400 7th St., SW
Washington, DC 20590

Motorists Assistance Directory
Ocean Highway Association
1768 Independence Blvd.
Virginia Beach, VA 23455
(A guide to aid for travelers between New York and Florida.
A map and a motorists' guidebook are also available.)

Open Your Eyes to Vision in Highway Safety
American Optometric Association
7000 Chippewa St.
St. Louis, MO 63119

Ryan's Gas Guide
RMS
P.O. Box 20995
Billings, MT 59104
(A guide to 1,200 discount gasoline stations.)

Safe Driving in Winter
U.S. Dept. of Transportation
National Highway Traffic Safety Administration
Washington, DC 20590

Shell Answer Books
P.O. Box 61609
Houston, TX 77208
(Booklets on many subjects, including *Emergency Repairs, Foul Weather Driving,* and *Driving Emergencies.* Also available from local dealers.)

Staying Alert on the Highway
Budget Rent-a-Car Corp.
35 E. Wacker Dr.
Chicago, IL 60601
(Fifteen illustrated exercises to relieve fatigue while driving.)

24-Hour Full-service Auto-Truck Stops Directory (Reymont Associates, 29 Reymont Ave., Rye, NY 10580)

Motoring in the USA
USA Travel Information
USA Travel Bargains
U.S. Travel Service
Department of Commerce
14th and Constitution Ave., NW
Washington, DC 20230

INSURANCE

AAA Worldwide Travel, Inc.
1712 G St., NW
Washington, DC 20006

American International Underwriters, Inc.
102 Maiden Lane
New York, NY 10005

MAPS

Free maps are available from:

Exxon Touring Service
P.O. Box 307
Florham Park, NJ 07932

P.O. Box 2180
Houston, TX 77001

Mobil Travel Bureau
P.O. Box 25
Versailles, KY 40383

Texaco Travel Service
P.O. Box 1459
Houston, TX 77001

These services will mark maps with suggested routes if you let them know where you plan to go.

Travel Tips, a booklet published by Exxon Touring Service, tells where to write in different states for free highway maps.

Ask your local Gulf dealer for the card you can mail in for a free ninety-six-page road atlas and travel guide.

RENTALS

U.S.

Check the listings under "Automobile Rental and Leasing" in your local Yellow Pages.

Europe

Avis Rent-a-Car
900 Old Country Rd.
Garden City, NY 11530
(Publishes the booklets *Car Facts* and *Common Rates in Europe in 1980.*)

Budget Rent-a-Car
35 E. Wacker Drive
Chicago, IL 60601
800–228–9650
(Publishes the booklet *Getting Around Overseas.*)

Europcar
National Car Rental
5501 Green Valley Dr.
Minneapolis, MN 55437
800–328–4567 (Minnesota and Canadian residents call 612–830–2345 collect)

Europe by Car
630 Fifth Ave.
New York, NY 10020

9000 Sunset Blvd.
Los Angeles, CA 90069

Other Foreign

Avis LAC Division
P.O. Box 343542
Coral Gables, FL 33134
800–331–2112
(Offers maps and self-drive tour brochures for Mexico, the Virgin Islands, Puerto Rico, Jamaica, and Guatemala.)

Budget Rent-a-Car
(see address above)
(Publishes the booklet *The Car Renter's Guide to Driving in Latin America and the Caribbean.*)

If you're planning to drive while in a non-English-speaking country, be sure to contact your local Automobile Association of America office to find out if you will need an international driver's

license. If you're going to Canada, call AAA about required proof
of insurance.

Bus

Motorcoach Tour Mart
Grace J. Talmage and Associates
Willow Grove, PA 19090

Check the listings under "Bus" in your local Yellow Pages. If
you have a complaint, contact the carrier or:

Interstate Commerce Commission
Public Information Office
12th St. and Constitution Ave.
Washington, DC 20423

Motor Homes

ASSOCIATIONS

Recreational Vehicle Industry Association
Box 204
Chantilly, VA 22021

BOOKS / MAGAZINES

RV Service and Repair Directory. Check your local library.
1980 RV Campground and Services Directory and *Trailer Life*
monthly magazine (Trailer Life Publishing Co., 29901 Agoura
Rd., Agoura, CA 91302)

RENTALS

Look under "Motor Homes—Renting or Leasing" in your
Yellow Pages or call AAA Motor Homes Rentals at the toll-free

number 800–453–5747.

Travelwide Queens Tours
580 Fifth Avenue
New York, NY 10036
(Information about renting Mercedes-Benz mobile homes in
Europe.)

Ship

B O O K S / P U B L I C A T I O N S

All About Voyages on Freighters and Cruise Ships (Harian Pub-
  lications, Floral Park, NY 11001)
Caribbean Hideaways by Ian Keown (Crown). Contains supple-
  ment on charter yachts.
Ford's Freighter Travel Guide and *Ford's International Cruise
  Guide* (Ford's Travel, Box 505, Woodland Hills, CA 91365)
The Freighter Cruise Quick Reference Guide (Air and Marine
  Travel Service, 501 Madison Ave., New York, NY 10022)
Klevens' Freighter Travel Letter (6500 Kelvin Ave., Canoga
  Park, CA 91306)

O T H E R   S O U R C E S   O F   I N F O R M A T I O N

Check listings under "Boats, Rental and Charter," "Cruises,"
and "Steamship Companies" in your local Yellow Pages.

Boat Enquiries Ltd.
7 Walton Well Rd.
Oxford OX2 6ED, England
(Provides brochures on cruises in narrowboats or converted
barges on the canals and rivers of Great Britain, France, Holland,
Denmark, Sweden, and Germany. These cruises can be in either
hotel-boats or self-drive boats.)

Camera Cruises
Box 387
Larchmont, NY 10538

Delta Queen Steamship Company
511 Main St.
Cincinnati, OH 45202
(Paddlewheel steamer information.)

Museums of fine arts

Natural history museums

The Smithsonian Institution
A & I 1278
Washington, DC 20560
202–381–5635

Traveltips Freighter Association
Box 933
Farmingdale, NY 11737
(Provides planning, reservations, and information on freighter cruises; puts out bimonthly publication.)

Train

UNITED STATES

Marketing Department
Amtrak
400 North Capitol, SW
Room 8060
Washington, DC 20006
800–523–5720

COMPLAINTS

Contact the carrier or:

Interstate Commerce Commission
Public Information Office
12th St. and Constitution Ave.
Washington, DC 20423

Auto-Train Corp.
Dept. E
1801 K St., NW
Washington, DC 20006

EUROPE

Baxter's Eurailpass Travel Guide by Robert Baxter (RailEurope,
    P.O. Box 3255, Alexandria, VA 22302)
Enjoy Europe by Train by William J. Dunn (Scribners, 1974)
Europe by Eurail (Box 20334, Columbus, OH 43220). Gives in-
    formation on train travel from European capitals, including
    many trips that can be made in a day.

Eurail Guide
Saltzman Companies
27540 Pacific Coast Highway
Malibu, CA 90265

Eurailpasses can be bought through a travel agent or by
writing:

Eurailpass
Box M
Staten Island, NY 10305

French National Railroads
610 Fifth Avenue
New York, NY 10020

Eurail covers rail travel in Austria, Denmark, Finland, France,
West Germany, Greece, Holland, Ireland, Italy, Luxembourg,
Norway, Portugal, Spain, Sweden, and Switzerland. It also covers
some bus and ferry travel, as well as travel on some lake and
river steamers.

Travel Agents

What Is a Travel Agent?
American Society of Travel Agents
711 Fifth Avenue
New York, NY 10022

The Travel Agent and You
Better Business Bureau of Metropolitan New York
275 Park Avenue S.
New York, NY 10016

22. PLANNING FOR GOING ABROAD

THE LURE of faraway places has tempted honeymooners and other travelers throughout the centuries. Oh, to discover the enchantment of Paris on a balmy summer evening . . . the mystery of the Casbah and the Moroccan desert . . . the lush native beauty which inspired Gauguin in Tahiti . . . the fascination of an ancient civilization such as that of China! The choices are rich and varied, from the leisure of basking in the sun on a tropical beach to actively exploring a totally different culture.

If you're experienced travelers and speak the language of the country you plan to visit, you may find a honeymoon in foreign climes a delightful beginning to married life. Traveling abroad isn't for everyone, though—at least as a honeymoon choice. Because you'll be experiencing so many new sensations and situations on any honeymoon trip, you'll want to consider carefully whether you should add the possible stresses of coping with a language and culture which are strange to you. Becoming acquainted with each other as marriage partners is a big adjustment in itself, so the comfort of a honeymoon site that isn't too exotic is often the best choice for this happy transition period. Foreign lands can be saved for a vacation later in your life together.

We've traveled throughout the United States as well as to a number of other countries, so we know the pleasures of both choices. Selecting the right location for your honeymoon is a very personal decision—and one that we hope will result in a trip filled with wonderful experiences for a lifetime of beautiful memories!

If you do intend to travel abroad, we've compiled a directory of information which may help in your planning and during your honeymoon to a foreign land.

Many countries maintain consulates and/or tourist bureaus in major cities throughout the United States. These can be very useful in providing you with a wide range of information about their countries. Check your local telephone book for those in your area (look in the Yellow Pages under "Governments— Foreign Representatives") or find out their addresses in New York City, where all countries in diplomatic relations with the United States have offices.

The U.S. State Department publishes several booklets which may provide useful background about other countries. *Your Trip Abroad* has information on passports, health requirements, and other aspects of overseas travel. It may be obtained from the U.S. Government Printing Office, Washington, DC 20402. *Background Notes on Countries of the World* is a series of pamphlets about a number of foreign nations. These may be ordered from the Office of Passport Services, Washington, DC 20524.

Customs

To help ease your way through customs inspections in the United States and other countries, you may want to order the following publications:

Know Before You Go

U.S. Customs
P.O. Box 7118
Washington, DC 20044
(Gives details of U.S. Customs regulations.)

GSP and the Traveler, which is also available from U.S. Customs (address above), details items that can be brought back from developing countries without any duty. GSP stands for Generalized Systems of Preferences.

Travelers' Tips

U.S. Department of Agriculture
Federal Building
Hyattsville, MD 20782
(Advises travelers on bringing food, plants, and animal products into the U.S.)

TIPS ABOUT CUSTOMS

Before purchasing any watches, cameras, tape recorders, or similar equipment—either before your trip or while abroad—it's advisable to check reports and ratings in publications such as *Consumer Reports* or *Popular Science.* These magazines should be available in your local library.

Whenever you leave the United States, be sure to register your camera, recorders, and the like with Customs *before* you leave. The same is true of foreign-made watches, clothing, and so forth.

Find out if the country you plan to visit has any restrictions on film and photographic or recording equipment entering or leaving the country. You can find out by contacting the national tourist bureau or consulate.

You can protect your film from damage caused by airport security machines by packing it in FilmShield, a triple-layered plastic bag lined with lead foil. This is available at most camera stores or by writing:

SIMA Products Corp.
7574 North Lincoln Avenue
Skokie, IL 60076

Eastman Kodak Co.
Department 841
343 State Street
Rochester, NY 14650
(Its booklets include *Tips for Photographing Your Trip Abroad*
(AC-17) and *Photography: How It Works* (AT-2).

Documenting Who You Are

Whether you're honeymooning in this country or abroad,
you'll need certain types of identification. Among the most important will be your driver's license (especially if you're from a
state that puts your photograph on the license), insurance identification (both personal and automobile, if you're driving), and
credit cards. Even if you've paid in advance or plan to pay in cash
or check at the end of your stay, your resort/hotel reservations
clerk may ask to see a credit card. This has become almost a
standard identification procedure in major U.S. cities.

Other documents you should take along, whether here or
abroad, include all correspondence and confirmations with hotels, airlines, trains, car-rental agencies, and so on. You'll also
want to record the numbers of your traveler's checks and credit
cards, as well as the emergency telephone number to call in
case of theft or loss. Keep both these records separate from the
traveler's checks and/or credit cards.

In fact, it's a good idea to leave a duplicate record of these
numbers with your travel agent, family, or a close friend, in case
of emergency. Keep all your documents together in an easily
accessible place—your travel agent may supply a special folder
for this purpose, or you could use a heavy-duty manuscript folder.

PASSPORTS

A passport is one of the most important documents for foreign travel. It establishes the identity of an individual and grants him or her permission to travel abroad. When traveling, do *not* pack your passport in your luggage—keep it on your person, preferably in an inside pocket. Don't give it to anyone except immigration authorities and, if required to do so, to hotel receptionists.

Never "lend" your passport or allow someone to hold it as collateral for a debt. If it's lost or stolen while you're abroad, report the loss immediately to the American Consulate. If it's damaged in some way it may be rendered invalid, so report any damage to your passport to the American Consulate right away. Take good care of your passport. If it's lost or damaged you'll have to go through a lot of inconvenience and explaining before you're issued a replacement.

Where to Apply

1. Any federal court clerk.
2. Clerk of any state court of record.
3. Judge or clerk of any probate court.
4. Clerks in certain designated post offices.
5. Agents at passport agencies in:

Boston	New York
Chicago	Philadelphia
Honolulu	San Francisco
Los Angeles	Seattle
Miami	Washington, DC
New Orleans	

If your passport has been issued within the past eight years, you may be able to obtain a new one by mail. Copies of the appropriate forms are available from the sources listed above.

If a passport is to be amended to include an additional person, it will be necessary to appear before an authorized passport agent. Amendments can be made by the Passport Office, Department of State, Washington, DC 20524; one of the passport agencies; American diplomatic and consular officers abroad; and the chief executive officers of the Commonwealth of Puerto Rico, Guam, the Virgin Islands, and American Samoa.

Losses

Should be reported immediately to:

Passport Office
Department of State
Washington, DC 20524

or

The nearest American consular office

To qualify for a passport, you have to present proof of citizenship, such as a birth certificate or baptismal certificate. You will also need identification with both your signature and a physical description or photograph. A previous passport, a permanent driver's license, or a government identification card or pass are considered good documentation. Processing will take three to five weeks.

You'll also need two identical (from the same negative) photographs taken within the last six months. You should sign both photographs on the front left-hand side, being careful not to write over the facial features. The photographs can be black-and-white or color, but must be no smaller than 2½ by 2½ inches, nor larger than 3 by 3 inches. They should be clear, front-view, full-face portraits on a light background. The paper must be thin and unglazed. Snapshots, vending-machine photos, and full-length shots aren't acceptable. The easiest solution is to go to a photographer who advertises passport photos.

The two of you aren't eligible for a joint passport until you're married, so you'll have to get individual passports, with the woman using her maiden name. Individual passports are preferable anyway, in case you become separated for some reason while traveling abroad, or if you must travel separately sometime in the future.

As soon as you get your passport, sign it as indicated. Until you do, it isn't valid.

VISAS

A visa is generally a stamped notation in a passport indicating that the bearer (meaning *you*) can enter a given country for a certain purpose and length of time. Some countries, but not all, require visas. Check with your travel agent or the consulate of any country you plan to visit about requirements. If you arrive without a visa you might be refused entry.

You can get your visas from the embassy or consulate of the country you're planning to visit. A minimum of forty-eight hours from the time of your application to approval is usual, and many nations take much longer. Since your passport must be submitted separately for each visa, you'll have to get organized very early if you're going to be visiting more than one country. Your travel agent, if you use one, can get your visa(s) for you or perhaps recommend a good visa service. These services can save you a lot of time and energy if you need more than one visa.

For more information write for:

Fees Charged by Foreign Countries for the Visa of United States Passports

Passport Office
Department of State
Washington, DC 20524

or contact the consulate or national tourist bureau of the appropriate country.

TOURIST CARDS

Tourist cards are required by some countries. You can find out whether you need one when you call or write to the foreign embassy about a visa.

If you're only visiting for a short time, many countries don't require either a visa or a tourist card, but you'll need to check in advance to make sure.

Electricity

Electric current and plugs vary from country to country, so if you'll be taking any electrical appliances on your wedding trip, be sure to take along a lightweight, all-purpose transformer and plug adapter. These can be bought in department and hardware stores and possibly at the airport. Check with the desk clerk at your hotel abroad to find out exactly what procedure to follow. For a booklet on the subject write:

Foreign Electricity Is No Deep Dark Secret
Franzus Co.
352 Park Ave. S.
New York, NY 10010

Guide Service

Personal sight-seeing service is available in Great Britain and Europe. These services can be arranged to accommodate special interests and needs, including those of handicapped travelers. For information, write:

Take-a-Guide Ltd.
63 E. 79th St.
New York, NY 10021
800–223–6450

Learning a Language

Even if you've been reassured that many people in the place(s) you'll be visiting speak English, take the time and the small amount of effort necessary to learn a few phrases in the local language, even if they're limited to "please," "thank you," and "you're welcome."

If you have trouble understanding someone's English, be patient and give him or her time. To people abroad, *English* is the foreign language. Most of all, go with the determination to enjoy the country and people and to learn as much as you can. This attitude will contribute amazingly to your honeymoon enjoyment.

For more information, try the following resources:

NATIONWIDE COMMERCIAL LANGUAGE SCHOOLS

Berlitz Schools Corporate Offices
Research Park—Building O
1101 State Rd.
Princeton, NJ 08540
609–921–0260

Inlingua School of Languages
551 Fifth Avenue
New York, NY 10022
212–682–8585

OTHER SOURCES

University adult-education programs (make sure the course emphasizes conversation and not literature)
Private tutors
Records and tapes

Legal Guidelines

Remember always that while you're in a foreign country you are subject to the same laws that apply to its own citizens. In researching your honeymoon destination, find out as much as possible about local customs and laws, and then respect them.

In some foreign countries, offenses that might not be too serious in the United States can be very serious indeed. Once there, if you feel that you may be arrested, consult the American Consulate immediately. Its staff will advise you and give you a list of lawyers. The consul can't act as your lawyer or obtain your release.

Use basic common sense to keep out of trouble. If you find yourself in the vicinity of a civil disturbance such as a demonstration or fight, leave the area immediately. Don't carry any messages, money, or packages into or out of any country for another person unless authorities of that country confirm that this does not break any laws. Don't carry or use "recreational" chemicals, and if you find yourself in a place where they're being used, leave as quickly and quietly as possible. Some countries also have strict laws governing the amount of their own or United States currency that you can bring in or take out.

Medical Precautions

If you're taking a packaged tour, it's advisable to buy an insurance policy that covers the cost of a ticket home if you must leave the tour for medical reasons.

If you have a chronic health problem, ask your doctor to prepare a short medical history. Be sure to include the generic names of any drugs you are taking. You can obtain a "Medical Passport," which includes space for your medical history and for the results of a recent physical examination and of laboratory tests, from the Medical Passport Foundation, 35 E. 69th St., New York, NY 10021.

Get a full supply of any medications you take regularly, and ask your doctor for a renewal prescription that uses generic terms. Be sure all medicine is properly labeled with the name of the drug, your name, and that of your physician.

If you have an American Express card, request a copy of that company's *Medical Payment Services Directory*, which lists facilities worldwide that accept American Express.

INFORMATION / BOOKLETS

Medifile
120 Boylston St.
Boston, MA 02116
(This service stores medical information on microfilm, which it can send to any part of the world within twenty-four hours.)

Intermedic, Inc.
777 Third Ave.
New York, NY 10017
(An international network of physicians who speak English and will respond in an emergency; a directory of participating physicians is available.)

International Association for Medical Assistance to Travelers
350 Fifth Avenue
New York, NY 10001
(Free directory of physicians throughout the world, plus information on climate and sanitary conditions in cities around the world.)

Family Health Record

Dept. of Health Education
American Medical Association
535 N. Dearborn St.
Chicago, IL 60610

Health Precautions for Foreign Travel

Dept. CB
P.O. Box 2382
Boston, MA 02107

IMMUNIZATION

Contact your local or state health department for information on immunizations required and recommended for different parts of the world.

Required immunizations must be recorded on approved forms. The authorized booklet *International Certificates of Vaccination* is available from most local health departments and passport offices.

Health Information for International Travel

U.S. Dept. of Health, Education and Welfare
Center for Disease Control
Bureau of Epidemiology
Atlanta, GA 30333

Depending on where you're going, the requirements of the World Health Organization may include vaccination or inoculation against smallpox, cholera, and yellow fever.

For return to the United States you'll need only a smallpox certificate, if in the preceding fourteen days you've visited a country reporting smallpox. However, many countries require entering travelers to possess a valid International Certificate of Vaccination against smallpox. You can often receive your inoculations free or at minimal charge from a local or state health clinic—check with them for details and recommendations of where to be immunized. When you receive your inoculations, it may be a wise precaution to have a tetanus shot or booster and a polio booster.

Do get your immunizations well in advance of your departure. One bride was told there would be "no side effects." She suffered such pain in reaction to one inoculation that she couldn't lift her arm for most of the trip. That's no way to spend your honeymoon!

IF YOU BECOME ILL WHILE ABROAD

U.S Consulates have lists of English-speaking doctors. You can also check with your hotel staff or local newspapers for the names of organized medical services. Large university or teaching hospitals generally have English-speaking doctors. U.S. military hospitals can offer only limited assistance to seriously ill travelers.

Note: Medicare provides very limited coverage, and only in Mexico and Canada.

If you must be treated for a medical emergency while away, be sure to get copies of any results of X rays or lab tests, or a treatment report (at least get the identifying number of the report). Note the name and telephone number of any doctor treating you and get a copy of an itemized bill. If you have X rays taken, be sure to find out when they will be ready, as well as the name of the person you or your doctor should call if there are any questions. Sign a permission form so your record can be sent to your own doctor.

How to Avoid Turista, Montezuma's Revenge, or Whatever It's Called Wherever You Are

- Drink only boiled or bottled water, coffee, tea, or beer.
- Boil any water you must drink.
- Don't forget that ice cubes are made from unboiled water.
- Avoid raw vegetables and salads, and fruits you can't peel.
- If you don't succeed and are stricken, try to replenish the liquids lost. A recommended treatment is a diet of tea, applesauce, and plain boiled rice.
- Recommended medications are Lomotil or paregoric. Ask your doctor about the antibiotic Vibramycin, available only by prescription.

Money Matters

If you're going abroad it might be a good idea to buy a package of mixed currency and coins of the place(s) you'll visit before you leave the United States. Sometimes called a Pre-Pak or Tip-Pak, such foreign-currency packages can be bought with the payment of a modest fee from most major banks or from many travel agents. The package usually includes a currency-conversion chart with pictures of the most commonly used bills and coins. You'll want at least enough foreign money to pay for transportation to your hotel, tips, and your first meal in case you can't get to a bank when you arrive at your destination. Of course, there usually are exchange centers in airports and major rail stations where foreigners arrive, but it won't hurt to have a little "cash on hand."

Some countries don't allow foreigners to bring in the local currency, requiring that you make all exchanges within the country. You probably won't have any trouble if you bring only a small amount of currency and don't flash it around or talk about it as you arrive. Whether you exchange money in advance or not, it's good to familiarize yourself with your destination country's denominations and their dollar equivalents.

Before you leave, change all your local coins into bills, except those you will need for tipping airport people. (You'll be stuck with any coins you bring back.) You will have to pay airport departure fees, usually, but you can always exchange extra bills for dollars once you get back to the U.S.

For a list of places to purchase foreign currency, including the prepackaged variety, and a list of exchange houses abroad, write:

The Deak Perera Group, Inc.
Dept. W
763 United Nations Plaza
New York, NY 10006

TIPS ON GETTING THE MOST FOR YOUR MONEY WHEN EXCHANGING IT

1. Make your exchange during normal business hours.
2. Do it at a bank or exchange house. Avoid exchanging money at airports, hotels, restaurants, stores, or train or bus stations.
3. Take a pocket calculator or currency converter with you. This will help you determine whether you're getting a reasonable rate.
4. Don't exchange too much at one time. But before departure, do be sure to set aside enough to cover airport taxes, taxi fares, tips, and so forth.
5. Try to cash as much as you need at any one time. Fewer transactions incur fewer fees.

6. On Friday, be sure you have enough to get you through the weekend.

For more information write for:

Guide to Rates and Currency Regulations

Republic National Bank
Banknote Department
Box 336
Midtown Station
New York, NY 10018

IF YOU LOSE OR RUN OUT OF MONEY OR TRAVELER'S CHECKS

Before leaving home, find out if your bank has a foreign office and can send you cash in foreign currency from your account.

If someone else must wire you money, request that he or she use a bank with a foreign office.

A letter of credit from your bank is a handy insurance policy.

Keep your list of the serial numbers of your traveler's checks separate from the checks themselves. It's also advisable to leave a copy of this list with someone at home in case yours gets lost or stolen. Most issuers will replace lost checks promptly, if you can produce the serial numbers. Act immediately when you discover the loss or theft.

Personal checks are generally not accepted. However, it is advisable to carry a couple of blanks with you for those rare occasions when a personal check will do the trick. For instance, the U.S. Customs will accept personal checks if you have two pieces of identification. American Express will also accept personal checks up to a certain amount if you present your American Express card.

Visa card holders can obtain cash advances at foreign banks.

The American Embassy will help you wire home for money. It will do no more; it will not lend you money, or cash personal checks.

CREDIT CARDS

Credit cards can spare you the nuisance of carrying around large amounts of cash or traveler's checks. They also enable you to draw on extra funds. Try to obtain a widely accepted credit card issued by a company that has many offices in the U.S. and abroad. Generally, to qualify for one, you need a stable job and an income of at least $10,000 a year, plus information and personal references establishing you as a good credit risk. Aside from its other advantages, a credit card allows you to pay for your purchases as much as a month later—after you return from your honeymoon.

While you can get by with one card, no single card is accepted everywhere—and many places don't accept them at all, especially abroad. If you're going to travel extensively, you may want more than one. (A caution: since too many credit cards can sometimes lure us to spend more than we can afford, consider carefully whether you really need extra cards.) If you'll be traveling in the U.S. as well as abroad, be aware that some major retail chains with their own nationwide cards take no outside cards. If you're going to drive a lot, you might want a card from your favorite oil company.

If your credit card is lost or stolen, report this to the credit-card company immediately, by telephone or telegram. You may also want to register all your credit cards with a central agency which will report theft or loss to all the companies for you. Check with your credit-card companies to learn whether they offer such a reporting service. You may also register your credit cards through the Airline Passengers Association (P.O. Box 2758, Dallas, TX 75221; 800–527–6006).

TRAVELER'S CHECKS

Traveler's checks are usually safer than currency. If they're stolen, they can be replaced. In addition, they're sometimes accepted in places that won't take a credit card.

The major sources of traveler's checks (see your local phone book for branches) are:

American Express	Bank America
Barclays	Local savings and loan institu-
Thomas Cook	tions
Deak-Perera	Other commercial banks
Citibank	

American Express, Barclays, Cook, Deak-Perera, and Bank of Tokyo issue traveler's checks in foreign currencies.

Traveler's checks can be charged to certain credit cards. However, there are ceilings on the amounts that can be charged.

When buying your traveler's checks, ask if the issuer has a toll-free number where you can report losses and apply for a refund. Also ask for the directory of offices where you can get a refund.

Every day, look through your checks to make sure that none have been stolen from the inside of the booklet. If any traveler's checks have been lost or stolen, report this to the local bureau of the issuing company. To avoid problems, keep the bulk of your traveler's checks in the hotel safe.

Some money tips

- Avoid winding up with unneeded foreign bills by taking along a supply of dollar bills for last-minute purchases.
- If you find yourself stuck with a handful of coins, you can turn them into a souvenir by having a jeweler drill holes in them and attach them to a charm bracelet.
- If you're worried about being stuck with counterfeit bills or coins, get the booklet *Know Your Money* from your local Secret Service office.

Telephone

Information on telephone rates and time differentials is contained in a series of booklets put out by AT&T. For copies, write:

"Getting Around Overseas"
AT&T Long Lines
110 Belmont Drive
Somerset, NJ 08873

The booklets also include addresses of U.S. embassies and consulates and lists of foreign words, measures, currency, and clothes-size conversions. Similar booklets are put out by Budget Rent-a-Car.

Calling home from a hotel in a foreign country can often add astronomical surcharges to your bill. The practice of adding surcharges has become so prevalent that AT&T has established a program called Teleplan. Cooperating hotels agree to limit extra charges to an additional $2 to $10, depending on the hotel, country, and final cost of the call. Having been caught in this surcharge trap (which can double, triple, or even quadruple the cost of an overseas call), we strongly advise checking your hotel's policy before placing such calls.

For options to the hotel surcharge, we suggest the following:

1. Make calls from a public telephone center. These are often located in the local post office and also in many airports and train stations.
2. Surcharges are usually based on a percentage of the total bill, so keep calls brief and ask your party to call you back.
3. Call collect or use a telephone credit card. Although you'll pay a service charge for the call, you'll avoid the surcharge.

23. A QUICK AND EASY GUIDE TO TIPPING

TIPPING is probably the most confusing item in travel etiquette. Even experienced travelers are sometimes uncertain about whom and how much to tip.

The custom originated as a reward for good service ("*To Insure Prompt Service*"), and should still be based on the quality of the service received. If it's poor, tip accordingly and explain why—you're *never* obligated to tip someone who's rude or inefficient or who disregards your instructions.

In general, tips are distributed as soon as a service is rendered; however, on a cruise ship or in a hotel or resort, tip the staff at the end of your stay (some travelers refer to the next-to-last day on a cruise as "Palm Sunday," for obvious reasons). In some cases (as we'll indicate later), you may want to give part of the tip in advance in order to be sure of special service.

Here are some of the current standards for tipping. Amounts may differ slightly owing to fluctuations in the economy. You can check with your travel agent, tour director, or the hotel/resort management about local customs regarding tipping.

Transportation

· *Taxi driver:* 25¢ for $1 or less; 15–20 percent of the fare over $1, plus tolls.
· *Airport bus driver:* Nothing.
· *Car-rental attendant:* Nothing.
· *Hotel limousine driver:* 10–15 percent of the fare (50¢ minimum).

- *Private limousine driver:* 10–15 percent of the fare.
- *Porters/skycaps* at bus or train station/airport: 50¢ per bag. (Tip dock porters 50¢ per bag even if "No Tipping" signs are posted—otherwise your baggage may sit on the dock all day.)
- *Bus driver/conductor* (package or charter tour): $5–$10 per day from entire tour group (if tip isn't included in tour price).
- *Airline:* No tipping on the plane.
- *Train sleeping-car attendant:* $1 each time your berth is made up; *dining-car waiter/waitress*—15 percent of bill; *dining-car attendant*—nothing.

Cruises: Generally totals about 5 percent of your basic passage. On short cruises—*waiter/waitress, cabin attendant*—$1.50–$2 per day; *dining-room and cabin attendant's assistant*—50¢–$1 per day. Even where there is a "no tipping" policy, it is customary to tip waiters/waitresses and cabin attendants at least $1 a day. On long cruises—$2 per day or $20–$25 per cabin per week is common for *waiters and attendants.* If the trip lasts a month or longer, tip every two or three weeks. *Maitre d'*—$5–$10 for special service. *Station captain or head attendant*—$5–$10 per person for a short cruise or $5–$10 per person per week for a longer cruise if you use his or her services frequently; $10 for a one-time special service. *Wine steward*—$5–$7 per person for a short cruise or per week for a longer cruise if you use his or her services regularly. *Bartenders, lounge attendants*—15–20 percent of the bill; *deck-chair attendants*—$1 a day on a short cruise, $5 a week on a longer one if you take chairs; *telephone operator* for ship-to-shore calls—$1–$2; *ship's officers, social director, customs officials*—nothing.

On *freighters*—ranges from $5 a week for *dining-room attendants* and $3–$4 a week for *cabin attendants* to $1 a day per *crew member* who serves you.

Hotel/Resort

- *Door attendant:* 25¢–50¢ per bag if carried to front desk; 25¢–$1 for hailing a cruising taxi (nothing if there's a taxi line in front of the hotel).

- *Bellhop:* $1 per person or couple if you are shown to your room; $2 if you have a lot of luggage; 50¢ each time you order a delivery of newspapers, cigarettes, or other non-food items.
- *Parking attendant:* 50¢.
- *Room service:* 10–15 percent of the bill (50¢ minimum).
- *Laundry/valet service:* 15 percent of bill for delivery; more for rush service (50¢ minimum).
- *Guest-room attendant:* $1.50 per day (if more than two days) or $12–$15 per couple per week. Leave in envelope with your room number and "housekeeper" written on the outside.
- *Dining-room staff:* American Plan (meals included), $4 per day per couple; busboy—$1 per day.
  Note: Some resorts include 10–15 percent for gratuities in your package price. In this case you may wish to leave something extra for the housekeeping or dining-room staff, but it isn't necessary. At some resorts, gratuities are included in the package price, and tipping is forbidden.
- *Barber:* 50¢ (or 15–20 percent for a men's hair stylist).
- *Hair stylist:* 15–20 percent.
- *Shampooer:* 50¢–$1.
- *Manicurist:* $1.
- *Shoeshine:* 25¢–35¢.
- *Social director:* Not necessary. If you really enjoyed or participated in most of the planned activities—$5 per week.
- *Photographer:* Nothing (this applies to any other business owner or professional person).
- *Florist delivery:* 50¢.
- *Special services:* Depends on service. For example, if you must have a special diet, you may want to speak to the chef or dietitian the first day and give him or her a $5 tip for the extra effort involved.

Restaurant

- *Waiter, waitress:* 15–20 percent of the check, regardless of whether it is day or night; the tip is based on the bill before the tax is added. *Sommelier* (wine steward)—10 percent of

the cost of the wine ($1 minimum). The cost of the wine is also included in the basic tip to the waiter or waitress. *Maitre d'* or *captain*—$1–$10, but only for special attention.
· *Coat/hat check:* 50¢.

Recreation/Entertainment

· *Beach/pool chair attendant:* $1 per day per couple.
· *Snack-bar waiter* at pool/beach/golf club: 50¢ per person for food; 15 percent of beverage check.
· *Locker attendant:* 50¢ per day or $2.50 per week per person.
· *Sports pro:* $5 for several private lessons.
· *Golf caddy:* $1–$2 per bag or 15 percent of greens fees.
· *Sporting-event usher:* 25¢ per person for reserved seats.
· *Sight-seeing guide:* $1 per couple for a half day; $2 for a full day (or check with travel agent or hotel staff about local customs).
· *Theater usher:* In U.S., nothing; in some European cities, tips are expected (check with travel agent or hotel ticket service about local custom).
· *Casino dealer:* 10 percent of winnings (if you lose, $1–$5 for the evening is optional). *Waitress*—for chips, $1; for drinks, 15 percent of bill; for cigarettes, change (25¢ maximum). In casinos where drinks and cigarettes are free for players, 25¢–50¢ is the minimum tip.
· *Nightclub maitre d':* $5 for an especially good table; *bartender* or *waiter*—15–20 percent of check; *washroom attendant*—25¢–50¢; *cigarette/flower vendor*—change or 25¢; *coatroom attendant*—50¢ per coat; *doorman*—for hailing taxi, 25¢; *parking attendant*—50¢.
· *Musicians:* For a special request, $5–$10 for orchestra leader; $1 for pianist or individual guitarist/violinist/accordionist.
· *Nightclub photographer:* Nothing (this person is a concessionaire).

24. ABOUT HEALTH
AND SAFETY

Jet Lag and Other Discomforts

Jet lag is a phenomenon that occurs when a traveler crosses several time zones in a relatively short period of time. More than one hundred body functions are affected by this disruption of the normal twenty-four-hour day-night cycle. Research indicates that the effects are more devastating when traveling from west to east than from east to west. Travelers heading from north to south and vice versa experience the routine fatigue of travel, not jet lag.

Each person's experience with jet lag is different. Some travelers never change their watches or their schedules; others simply ignore the problem. It may take your body anywhere from two days to two weeks to get back to normal.

Here are several suggestions that may aid you in coping with jet lag:

PRE-DEPARTURE

1. Reset your internal clock by rearranging your sleeping schedule for several days prior to departure. If you're flying west, go to bed an hour later each evening and arise an hour later in the morning. If you're going in the opposite direction, go to bed an hour earlier each evening and arise an hour earlier the next day. Do this until your schedule corresponds to that of the place you'll be visiting. Rearrange your eating schedule accordingly.

This is the most drastic solution and may not be very practical. The following suggestions are more easily accomplished.

2. Try to arrange your flight so that you arrive at your destination in the evening.
3. Get plenty of rest the night before your departure.
4. Arrive at the airport in plenty of time so you won't be hassled before departure.

EN ROUTE

1. Wear loose, comfortable clothes.
2. Wear sandals; sprinkle powder in your shoes or take them off.
3. Eat lightly. You don't have to take advantage of all the food the airline serves.
4. Drink plenty of liquids, but keep alcoholic beverages to a minimum. Alcohol adds to the dehydration problem created by the lack of humidity in the plane.
5. Avoid smoking and the smoking section. Smoking decreases the oxygen-carrying capacity of the blood and promotes fatigue. Exposure to smoke can adversely affect the non-smoker.
6. Try to sleep.
7. Move around; keep your circulation going. Do isometric exercises; try a few deep knee bends.
8. Just before landing, refresh yourself by brushing your teeth and splashing cold water on your face.
9. If your destination is ten or more hours' flying time away, consider making the trip in two stages, with a day of rest in between.

ON ARRIVAL

1. If you've arrived in the morning and want to nap, don't allow yourself to sleep much beyond noon. Try to adapt to the new country's schedule as quickly as possible.

2. Save hectic sight-seeing or important appointments until the day after arrival.

3. Some travelers recommend hot baths; others, a set of tennis or some jogging. A number of travelers have reported that grapefruit juice on arrival (they bring along a couple of small cans with peel-off openings) works like a charm.

BOOKLETS

The Flight Safety Foundation and the Federal Aviation Administration have prepared a booklet called *Human Factors in Long Distance Flights.*

Disabled Travelers

AIR

The Federal Aviation Administration requires that airlines establish special procedures for passengers who would need assistance during a flight emergency. Check your airline for specifics.

TWA has a booklet, *Air Travel for the Handicapped,* available at TWA ticket offices. United also has a booklet, *Travel for the Handicapped.* For this, write:

Director of Consumer Affairs
United Airlines
P.O. Box 66100
Chicago, IL 60666

Another publication is *Access Travel: A Guide to the Accessibility of Airport Terminals.* For this, write:

Airport Operators Council International
1700 K St., NW
Washington, DC 20006

BOOKS

Travelability: A Guide for Physically Disabled Travelers in the United States by Lois Reamy (Macmillan, 1978).
The Wheelchair Traveler (22480 Cass Ave., Woodland Hills, CA 91364).
Lists sightseeing attractions.
Where Turning Wheels Stop (Paralyzed Veterans of America, 3636 16th St., NW, Washington, DC 20010). Rates accessibility of motels, hotels, restaurants.

For a catalog of guidebooks to major cities and national parks written for disabled travelers, write:

Director
Education and Information Service
Easter Seal Society for Crippled Children and Adults
Chicago, IL 60612

TOURS

Evergreen Travel Service
19492 44th Ave. W.
Lynnwood, WA 98036

Handy-Cap Horizons
3250 E. Loretta Dr.
Indianapolis, IN 46227

Tours for the Deaf
Embassy Travel
247 S. County Rd.
Palm Beach, FL 33480

Wheelchair Traveler
P.O. Box 169
Woodland Hills, CA 91364

TRAINS

Amtrak has special toll-free numbers for deaf persons who have access to a teletypewriter. They are:

800–523–6590 (outside of Pennsylvania)
800–562–6960 (Pennsylvania)

TRAVELING ABROAD

Be sure to tell the national tourist bureau about your disability. Many of these bureaus have special publications or fact sheets with information geared toward your needs. One such publication is *Access in Norway,* available from Central Council for the Disabled, 34 Eccleston Sq., London SWl, England.

Security

"Use your common sense" is the sagest advice anyone can give you when it comes to matters of security while traveling. Here are some tips proffered by the experts:

IN A HOTEL

- Use the hotel's safe-deposit box.
- Don't leave valuables in the open in your room.
- Don't flash lots of jewelry or money. Better still, leave your valuable jewelry at home.
- When you leave your room, hang out the "Do Not Disturb" sign, leave a light on, and leave the television or radio going. If you're out late in the evening, it's better to leave a network station on; it is apt to remain on the air later than local stations.
- Don't advertise your room number. Consider asking the desk clerk to verify any would-be visitors or telephone callers by calling you first, rather than giving out your room number or key.
- Don't open the door without first determining who's on the

other side. If you haven't called Room Service, don't open for someone announcing, "Room Service." Hotel employees will carry identification.

· Report any suspicions or incidents to hotel security.
· Don't leave your key or passcard (for new "keyless" locks now in many hotels) with the desk clerk; keep it with you. Don't leave it in the door, on the coffee-shop counter, or anyplace where it's accessible to others.
· Use all the available locks when sleeping or showering.
· When checking in and out, keep a close watch on your luggage.
· Recheck your valuables each time you return to your room.
· Make sure all doors and windows are locked when you leave —even if you'll only be gone for a few minutes.
· If you must keep money in the room, put it in several different spots: in the pockets of skirts or pants hanging up; between the pages of a newspaper, magazine, or book; inside a sheet of paper in a sealed addressed envelope that's out in the open with other letters and postcards.

OUT ON THE STREET, OUTSIDE YOUR ROOM

· Carry money in two wallets, a money belt, or your bra.
· Men should never carry their wallets in their hip pockets. Place the wallet, which has been emptied of all extraneous materials, in an inside jacket pocket and clip the pocket with a safety pin.
· Women should carry their pocketbooks on the side away from the street, under their arm and with any flaps toward the body. They should keep as far away from the curb as possible.
· Men can also place their valuables in a small bag suspended on a strap that is hung around the neck. The strap should be long enough so that the pouch can be tucked underneath the shirt and pants.
· Women can also hide their pocketbooks inside shopping bags.
· In general, carry only as much cash as is needed on any given

day. Use credit cards or traveler's checks whenever possible.
- Bring as little luggage as possible. The fewer pieces you have, the easier it is to keep track of them.
- Keep your valuables with you. Don't pack them in luggage that you check through.
- If you are robbed, inform the police immediately. If you are abroad, go to the nearest U.S. Consulate. Here you can get a new passport if yours has been stolen, as well as advice on replacing traveler's checks, airline tickets, and so forth.

Suggestions for Extra Precautions

- Pack a small hardwood wedge. You can place this under your hotel door to deter intruders who can manipulate the locks.
- A number of safety devices are available in department stores. Among them are burglar-alarm clocks, hangers with locking compartments for storing valuables, portable safes, and portable metal door wedges.

ON THE HOME FRONT

- Have someone check your house or apartment daily while you're gone.
- Don't publish the announcement of your wedding until after your return.
- Stop mail, milk, and newspaper deliveries and garbage pick-up, if you've already started these services.
- Leave with a relative or friend a house key, travel intinerary, list of emergency phone numbers, list of traveler's check numbers and credit card numbers, and inventory of what you've packed.
- Disconnect all electrical appliances and turn off all gas jets, including the jet for the hot-water heater.
- Store all valuables. Lock all doors and windows. Notify the local police that you will be away.
- Arrange for night lighting or set electric timers. Make arrangements for the care of pets, house plants, lawn.
- Empty the refrigerator.
- Eliminate possible fire hazards.

25. ABOUT LUGGAGE

Buying Luggage

Selecting Luggage
Consumer Information Center
Pueblo, CO 81009

The Traveler's Guide to Luggage
300 E. 44th St.
New York, NY 10017

Check *Consumer Reports* for the most recent ratings and recommendations.

Caring for Luggage

- *Smooth leather:* Use saddle soap, then rub with a paste wax or neutral shoe cream. Mink oil is a good conditioner to use if the leather appears dry. If you want to darken the leather, use lemon oil.
- *Vinyls and other plastics:* Use soap and water or special cleaners made for vinyls. You might want to wipe with a liquid wax to protect the surface.
- *Colored leather:* Use mild soapsuds; rub gently. Use a neutral shoe cream to preserve the leather.
- *Rawhide leather:* Use mild soapsuds; dampen but don't wet. For deep spots use fine steel wool.
- *Fabrics coated with stain repellent or clear plastic:* Use soap and water. Sponge on, rinse off, and dry. Use two tablespoons

of ammonia in one pint of water to remove heavy spots. A light application of liquid wax will preserve the surface.

· *Uncoated fabrics:* Use a light application of soap and water. For stains, use a spot remover. Coat with stain- or water-repellent spray to extend the life of the luggage.
· *Fiberglass:* Use soap and water. Remove scratches and scuffs with fine steel wool. Rinse thoroughly.
· *Metal:* Use the cleaning solvent appropriate for the particular metal.
· *Hardware:* Use steel wool for scratches or rust; reseal with lacquer or clear nail polish. Do not use oil.
· *Lining:* Use the cleansing agent called for by the fabric content and the manufacturer's instructions. If soap and water can be used, use as little as possible in order to prevent mildew. Dry thoroughly before closing.
· *Zippers:* Should be closed when storing luggage. Rub a beeswax candle over them if they become difficult to operate. Be sure your luggage is completely dry both inside and out before storing it. Store in an upright position away from extremes in temperature and humidity. To save space, you can store smaller pieces inside larger ones. Leather luggage needs air circulation for "breathing." You can further protect your non-leather luggage by using fitted covers or plastic or paper wrappings.

Lost or Damaged Luggage

AIRLINE PROCEDURE

1. Report the loss or damage immediately.
2. Don't surrender your baggage claim checks until you receive your bags. Make sure airline staff fills out a loss or damage report.
3. File a claim. If you don't receive a claim form from the carrier within two weeks of your reporting the loss or damage, request a claim form in writing. File your claim within forty-five days.

If you have a complaint, write:

Civil Aeronautics Board
Office of the Consumer Advocate
Washington, DC 20428

The limit on liability is $750. If your baggage is worth more, you can obtain additional coverage by declaring the excess value and paying a fee.

LOCATOR SERVICE

International Luggage Locator Service
5050 Excelsior Blvd.
Minneapolis, MN 55416
800–328–3890

TO REDUCE RISK OF LOSS OR DAMAGE

1. Arrive at the airport ahead of time.
2. Put your name, address, and telephone number on the inside and outside of each piece of luggage.
3. Mark your luggage with a distinctive tag or mark for ease of recognition.
4. Discard baggage checks from previous trips.
5. Don't overpack. The standard rule of thumb is: if you have to sit on your suitcase, it is overpacked.
6. Lock your luggage.
7. Make sure the ticket clerk fills out the tag correctly and attaches it securely. A tag slipped over the hanger top of hang-up luggage is not securely fastened; ask the clerk to attach the tag to a zipper or handle.
8. Don't ship your bags all the way through if you have to switch planes. Check the baggage through to the first stop, then check it through to the next stop.
9. Check your homeowners insurance policy to see if luggage losses are covered. Consider buying a short-term policy to cover all your personal belongings during the trip.

10. Your identification tag won't fall off (or be torn off) if you attach it with the split-ring type of key chain.

If you're going to Florida, Eastern Airlines has a Ship-Ahead Service. Eastern will pick up your luggage at your home and deliver it to your destination in Florida. For information, call an Eastern Air Freight Office or write:

Eastern Airlines
Ship-Ahead Service
MIAKP
Miami International Airport, FL 33148

Packing

Samsonite puts out a *Travelers Handbook* which tells how to pack compactly and easily and yet leave clothes wrinkle-free. Western International Hotels' booklet *Tips for the Woman Business Traveler* also contains packing information, as do booklets available from some airlines.

26. ADDITIONAL READING

General

MAGAZINES

Better Homes and Gardens Brides' Book
Brides
Modern Bride
Woman's Day Brides' Handbook

BOOKS/BOOKLETS

Bride's Guide to Successful Marriage Today (Condé Nast Publications)

The Eternal Bliss Machine by Marcia Seligson (Morrow, 1973)

Marriage by Robert O. Blood, Jr. (The Free Press, 1978)

Better Times edited by Frances Cerra (Doubleday Dolphin Book, 1975)

OTHER

Your telephone book, particularly the Yellow Pages
Your local newspaper
Public libraries
Universities

What's in a name?

Should the bride adopt the bridegroom's name, or should she retain her maiden name? For information on this subject, write:

Center for a Woman's Own Name
261 Kimberly
Barrington, IL 60010

A True Aphrodisiac: Good Health

BOOKS/BOOKLETS

Be Well by Mike Samuels (Random House, 1975)
The Best Health Ideas I Know by Robert Rodale (Avon, 1975)

Between You and Me by Drs. Barbara A. Gilchrist, Thomas B. Fitzpatrick, and John A. Parrish (Little, Brown, 1978)

The Complete Book of Good Health by Phoebe Phillips and Pamela Hatch (Crowell, 1978)

Essentials of Healthier Living by Justus Julius Schifferes (Wiley, 1972)

Feeling Good by Sara D. Gilbert (Four Winds, Scholastic Book Service, 1978)

Foreign Travel Immunization Guide by Hans H. Neumann (Medical Economics, 1978)

The Habits of Health by Donald Norfolk (Avon, 1978)

Headache by James W. Lance, M.D. (Scribners, 1975)

The Headache Book by Arnold P. Friedman, M.D. and Shervert H. Frazier, Jr., M.D., with Dodi Schultz (Dodd, Mead, 1978)

Health by John LaPlace (Prentice-Hall, 1976)

Health for Effective Living by Edward B. Johns (McGraw-Hill, 1975)

Health Now by Stephen Gray and Hollis N. Matson (Macmillan, 1976)

Healthful Living by Harold Diehl and Willard Dalrymple (McGraw-Hill, 1973)

Healthier Living Highlights by Justus Julius Schifferes and Louis J. Peterson (Wiley, 1975)

Herbal Guide to Inner Health by Jeanne Rose (Grosset & Dunlap, 1978)

The Holistic Way to Health and Happiness by Harold H. Bloomfield and Robert Kory (Simon & Schuster, 1978)

How Long Will I Live? and 434 Other Questions Your Doctor Doesn't Have Time to Answer and You Can't Afford Not to Ask by Lawrence Galton (Macmillan, 1976)

How to Save Your Life by Earl Ubell (Harcourt Brace Jovanovich, 1973; in paperback, Penguin, 1976)

Lifeplan for Your Health by Donald Vickery (Addison-Wesley, 1978)

Little-known Secrets of Health and Long Life by Steve Prohaska (Avco, 1972)

Living Longer and Better by Harold Elrick (World Publications, 1978)

The Massage Book by George Downing and Anne Kent Rush (Random House & The Bookworks, 1972)

More Than Two Aspirin: Hope for Your Headache Problem by Sey-- mour Diamond, M.D., and William Barry Furlong (Follett, 1976; in paperback, Avon, 1977)

The "Ms." Medical Guide to a Woman's Health by Cynthia W. Cooke, M.D., and Susan Dworkin (Doubleday, 1979)

My Body My Health by F. H. Stewart *et al.* (Wiley Medical, 1979). For women.

An Osteopathic Doctor's Treasury of Health Secrets by John E. Up- ledger, D.O. (Prentice-Hall, 1976)

The Power of Total Living by Marcus Bach (Dodd, Mead, 1977; in paperback, Fawcett, 1978)

Rx: How to Travel the World and Stay Healthy by James E. Banta, M.D., M.P.H., and Patrick J. Doyle, M.D., M.P.H. (Acropolis)

Ways of Health by David J. Sobel (Harcourt Brace Jovanovich, 1979)

Weathering: How the Atmosphere Conditions Your Body, Your Mind, Your Moods—and Your Health by Stephen Rosen, Ph.D. (M. Evans, 1979)

Well-being edited by Barbara Salat and David Copperfield (Double- day, 1979)

The Whole Health Catalogue by Shirley Motter Linde (Rawson Wade, 1978)

A Year of Beauty and Health by Beverly and Vidal Sassoon (Simon & Schuster, 1979)

You and Your Health by William Fassbender (Wiley, 1980)

Your Health Is What You Make It by C. W. Whitmoyer (Banner- Exposition, 1972)

Adult Physical Fitness, A Program for Men and Women
   Supt. of Documents
   U.S. Government Printing Office
   Washington, DC 20402

Basic Bodywork for Fitness and Health
   American Medical Association Order Unit
   535 N. Dearborn St.
   Chicago, IL 60610

Beyond Diet . . . Exercise Your Way to Fitness and Heart Health
   Mazola Nutrition Information Service
   Box 307
   Coventry, CT 06238

Exercise in the Chair
  SAS Airlines
  630 Fifth Ave.
  New York, NY 10020

Four Steps to Weight Control
  Health & Welfare Division
  Metropolitan Life Insurance Co.
  1 Madison Ave.
  New York, NY 10010

How to Shape Up and Keep in Shape
  Dept. of Citrus
  State of Florida
  Florida Citrus Commission
  Lakeland, FL 33802

Shaping Up for the Long Run
  Dept. SU-AE
  P.O. Box 207
  Coventry, CT 06238

Sitting Fit
  Westinghouse
  Architectural Systems Division
  4300 36th St., S.E.
  Grand Rapids, MI 49508

Successful Jogging
  Consumer Information Center
  Dept. 576-F
  Pueblo, CO 81009

A Foreign Language Guide to Health Care
  Public Relations
  Blue Cross and Blue Shield of Michigan
  600 Lafayette E.
  Detroit, MI 48226

Panic/or Plan?
  Health and Welfare Division
  Metropolitan Life Insurance Co.
  1 Madison Ave.
  New York, NY 10010
(This is a medical emergency guide. Metropolitan offers other book-

lets, including *Emergency Medical Identification, Home Nursing Handbook, You and Your Health,* and *Your Health and Your Driving.*)

M E D I C A L

Medical identification devices generally advise those giving emergency treatment about the wearer's special medical conditions or allergies. For information, ask your physician or write:

American Medical Association
535 N. Dearborn St.
Chicago, IL 60610

or

Medic Alert Foundation
Turlock, CA 95380

S L E E P

The Dream Makers by Richard Corriere and Joseph Hart (Funk & Wagnalls, 1977)
Manwatching: A Field Guide to Human Behavior by Desmond Morris (Harry N. Abrams, 1977)
Sentics: The Touch of Emotions by Dr. Manfred Clynes (Doubleday, 1978)
Sleep Positions, the Night Language of the Body by Samuel Dunkell, M.D. (William Morrow, 1977)

S T R E S S

Everything You've Always Wanted to Know About Energy but Were Too Weak to Ask by Naura Hayden (Hawthorn Books, 1977)
The Stress of Life by Hans Selye (McGraw-Hill Paperbacks, 1978)

Trousseau: His and Hers

GENERAL RESOURCES

A Travel and Fashion Guide
Consumer Service Division
Dept. TG2
International Ladies' Garment Workers' Union
22 W. 38th St.
New York, NY 10018

Traveler's Checklist
Cornwall Bridge Rd.
Sharon, CT 06069
(A catalogue of traveler's aids.)

Your Clothing Dollar
Money Management Institute
Household Finance Corp.
Prudential Plaza
Chicago, IL 60601

Fashion magazines

Major department stores

Specialty clothing stores

Planning a Family?

ASSOCIATIONS

American Fertility Society
1801 Ninth Ave. S.
Birmingham, AL 35205

Association for Population/Family Planning Libraries and Information Centers, International
165 Second Ave.
Clarion, PA 16214

Association for Voluntary Sterilization, Inc.
708 Third Ave.
New York, NY 10017

Association of Planned Parenthood Physicians
810 Seventh Ave.
New York, NY 10019

Birthright National Headquarters
62 Hunter St.
Woodbury, NJ 08096

Ladies Center, Inc.
Sex, Health Education Center
12550 Biscayne Blvd.
N. Miami, FL 33181
800–327–9880

Montreal Health Press, Inc.
P.O. Box 1000, Station G
Montreal, Quebec, Canada H2W 2N1
(Free *Birth Control Handbook.*)

National Alliance for Optional Parenthood
3 N. Liberty St.
Baltimore, MD 21201
(Pamphlets include *Am I Parent Material?* and *Parenthood Is Optional/or Is It.*)

The National Foundation/March of Dimes
Box 2000
White Plains, NY 10602
(Provides information on genetic counseling.)

Planned Parenthood Federation of America
810 Seventh Ave.
New York, NY 10019
(Pamphlets include *Basics of Birth Control, Birth Control—All the Methods That Work and the Ones That Don't, Condom, Foam Facts, All About Vasectomy.* 25¢ each)

Zero Population Growth Inc.
1346 Connecticut Ave., NW
Washington, DC 20036

BOOKS / BOOKLETS

Becoming Parents: Preparing for the Emotional Changes of First-time Parenthood by Sandra Sohn Jaffe and Jack Virtel (Atheneum)

Birth Control by Tarvez Tucker (Tobey, 1975)

Contraception, Abortion, Pregnancy by Alice Fleming (Thomas Nelson, 1974)

Contraceptive Technology 1978–1979 by Robert A. Hatcher, M.D. *et al.* (Irvington, 1979)

The Doctor's Case Against the Pill by Barbara Seaman (Wyden)

How to Have Intercourse Without Getting Screwed by Jennifer Harper Wear (Madrona, 1976)

Reproduction, Sex and Preparation for Marriage by Lawrence Q. Crawley (Prentice-Hall, 1973)

Sex and Birth Control by James Lieberman and Ellen Peck (Schocken Books, 1975)

Taking Chances: Abortion and the Decision Not to Contracept by Kristin Luker (University of California Press, 1978)

Women and the Crisis in Sex Hormones by Barbara Seaman and Gideon Seaman, M.D. (Rawson, Wade, 1978)

Contraception: Comparing the Options
U.S. Dept. of Health, Education and Welfare
Public Health Service
Office of Public Affairs
5600 Fishers Lane
Rockville, MD 20857

Setting the Stage for Intimate Moments

BOOKS

The Kiss (University Books, 1976)
The Pleasure Book by Julius Fast (Stein & Day, 1977)

ENVIRONMENTAL RECORDINGS

For the names of environmental recordings, consult the Schwann, Harrison, and other record and tape catalogs at your favorite record store or department.

What About Sex?

BOOKS

Androgyny: Toward a New Theory of Sexuality by June Singer (Anchor Press/Doubleday, 1977)

Any Woman Can! by David R. Reuben, M.D. (Bantam, 1972)

Be Good to Your Body by Trent Busby (Citadel Press, 1977)

Becoming Orgasmic: A Program of Sexual Growth for Women by Julia R. Heiman, Ph.D., Joseph LoPiccolo, Ph.D., and Leslie LoPiccolo, M.S. (Prentice-Hall, 1976)

Better Sex, Better Marriage by Robert F. Kaufmann (Morrow, 1978)

Between Consenting Adults by Cathrina Bauby (Macmillan, 1973)

Beyond the Male Myth: What Women Want to Know About Men's Sexuality, a National Survey by Anthony Pietropinto, M.D., and Jacqueline Simenauer (Times Books, 1977)

Beyond Sex-role Stereotypes: Readings Toward a Psychology of Androgyny edited by Joan P. Bean and Alexandra G. Kaplan (Little, Brown, 1977)

Body Liberation by Emily Coleman and Betty Edwards (J. P. Tarcher, 1977)

The Book of Love by David G. Delvin, M.D. (St. Martin's Press, 1977)

Coming Together, Coming Apart by Dr. Jay Kuten (Macmillan, 1974)

Cosmopolitan's Love Book by Helen Gurley Brown (Wilshire, 1978)

Dilemmas of Masculinity: A Study of College Youth by Mirra Komarovsky (Norton, 1976)

For People Who Make Love by John J. Secondi (Taplinger, 1975)

For Yourself: The Fulfillment of Female Sexuality by Lonnie Garfield Barbach (Doubleday, 1975)

Good Sex: The Healthy Man's Guide to Sexual Fulfillment by Gary Kelly (Harcourt Brace Jovanovich, 1979)

Healthy Sexuality by Donald A. Read (Macmillan, 1979)

The Hite Report by Shere Hite (Macmillan, 1976)

Human Sex and Sexuality by Edwin Benzel Steen (Wiley, 1977)

Human Sexual Inadequacy by Virginia E. Johnson and Dr. William H. Masters (Little, Brown, 1970)

The Illustrated Manual of Sex Therapy by Helen Singer Kaplan, M.D., Ph.D. (Quadrangle: Times Books, 1975)

Introduction to Human Sexuality by Bernard Goldstein (McGraw-Hill, 1975)

The Joy of Being a Woman . . . and What a Man Can Do by Ingrid Hult Trobish (Harper & Row, 1975)

The Joy of Sex by Alex Comfort, Ph.D. (Crown, 1972)

The Key to Feminine Response in Marriage by Ronald M. Deutsch (Ballantine, 1976)

The Liberated Man by Warren Farrell (Random House, 1975; in paperback, Bantam)

Love and Orgasm: A Revolutionary Guide to Sexual Fulfillment by Alexander Lowen, M.D. (Collier Books, 1975)

The Loving Book by James Trussell and Steve Chandler (New American Library)

The Male Machine by Marc Feigen Fasteau (McGraw-Hill, 1974)

Marital Therapy by Neil Jacobson with Gayla Margolin (Brunner/Mazel, 1979)

The Marriage and Family Book by Ravi Dass and Aparna (Schocken Books, 1978)

Men: A Book for Women edited by James Wagenvoord (Avon, 1978)

More Joy of Sex by Alex Comfort, Ph.D. (Simon & Schuster, 1975)

The Natural Way to Sexual Health by Henry G. Bieler (Charles Publications, 1972)

The New Sex Therapy by Helen Singer Kaplan, M.D., Ph.D. (Brunner/Mazel, 1974)

Our Bodies, Ourselves, a Book by and for Women by the Boston Women's Health Collective, Inc. (Simon & Schuster, 1976)

The Redbook Report on Female Sexuality by Susan Sadd and Carol Tavris (Delacorte Press, 1977)

Relationships by Steve Berman and Vivien Weiss (Hawthorn, 1978)

Sex for Women by Carmen Kerr (Grove, 1978)

Sex in Human Loving by Eric Berne (Pocket, 1971)

Sex Therapy at Home by David J. Kass and Fred F. Stauss (Simon & Schuster, 1976)

Sexual Awareness by Fred A. Johnson, Barry W. McCarthy, and Mary Ryan (Scrimshaw/Boyd & Fraser, 1975)

Sexual Loving by Joseph and Lois Bird (Doubleday, 1977)

Sexual Myths and Fallacies by James Leslie McCary (Schocken Books, 1973)

Sexual Pleasure in Marriage by Jerome and Julia Rainer (Simon & Schuster, 1969)

The Sexual Self by Dr. Avoda K. Offit (Ballantine, 1978)

Sexuality and Man by the Sex Information and Educational Council of the U.S. (Scribner's)

Toward a Psychology of Being by A. H. Maslow (Van Nostrand, 1968)

Understanding Human Sexual Inadequacy by Fred Belliveau and Lin Richter (Little, Brown). "Translators" of Masters and Johnson for the lay person.

Winning the Age Game by Gloria Heidi (Doubleday, 1976; in paperback, Addison-Wesley, 1977)

Woman's Orgasm: A Guide to Sexual Satisfaction by Benjamin Graber, M.D., and Georgia Kline-Graber, R.N. (Bobbs-Merrill, 1975)

COUNSELING

American Association of Marriage and Family Counselors
225 Yale Ave.
Claremont, CA 91711

American Association of Sex Educators, Counselors and Therapists
Suite 304
5010 Wisconsin Ave., NW
Washington, DC 20016

Association of Couples for Marriage Enrichment, Inc.
459 S. Church St.
Box 1596
Winston-Salem, NC 27108

Eastern Association of Sex Therapists
10 E. 88th St.
New York, NY 10028

For a clinic approved by Masters and Johnson, write:

Human Sexuality Center
Long Island–Jewish–Hillside Medical Center
410 Lakeville Rd.
New Hyde Park, NY 11040

or

Reproductive Biology Research Foundation
4910 Forest Park Blvd.
St. Louis, MO 63108

National Council on Family Relations
1219 University Ave., SE
Minneapolis, MN 55414

In a number of cities, there are specialized telephone services that answer callers' questions about sex.

Your local university or medical school may conduct a course on human sexuality.

Be sure to check a therapist's references and credentials carefully. The business is rife with rip-off artists.

Getting to Know One Another

BOOKS

The Art of Loving by Eric Fromm (Harper & Row, 1974)

Be Good to Each Other: An Open Letter on Marriage by Carol and Lowell Erdahl (Hawthorn Books, 1976)

The Dance-away Lover by Daniel Goldstine, Hilary Goldstine, Katherine Larner, and Shirley Zuckerman (William Morrow, 1978)

Dr. Knox's Marital Exercise Book by Dr. David Knox (David McKay)

Encounter: Love, Marriage and Family by Ruth E. Albrecht and E. Wilbur Bock (Holbrook Press, 1975)

Equal Marriage by Richard Bright and Jean Stapleton (Abingdon Press, 1976)

The Fragile Bond: Marriage Now by Ruth Winter (Macmillan, 1976)

Freedom and Growth in Marriage by James Leslie McCary (Wiley, 1980)

The Future of Marriage by Jesse Bernard (Bantam, 1973)

How to Be a Happily Married Mistress by Lois Bird (Doubleday, 1970)

How to Be Outrageously Successful With Women by John Mack Carter and Lois Wyse (Morrow, 1976)

How to Enjoy the Love of Your Life by Harold H. Bloomfield, M.D. (Doubleday, 1979)

How to Get Whatever You Want Out of Life by Dr. Joyce Brothers (Simon & Schuster, 1978)

How to Give and Receive Advice by Gerald I. Nierenberg (Simon & Schuster, 1975)

How to Live With Another Person by David S. Viscott, M.D. (Arbor House, 1974)

How to Succeed in Business and Marriage—For Men Only by Richard W. Ogden (American Management Association Inc., 1978)

The Liberated Man by Warren Farrell (Random House, 1975)

The Male Machine by Marc Feigen Fasteau (McGraw-Hill, 1974)

Marriage: Who? When? Why? by Dr. David Knox (Prentice-Hall, 1974)

No-fault Marriage by Marcia Lasswell and Norman Lobsenz (Double-day)

Oh Promise Me but Put It in Writing by Paul P. Ashley (McGraw-Hill, 1978)

Passages by Gail Sheehy (E. P. Dutton, 1976)

Personal Marriage Contract by John F. Whitaker, M.D. (OK Street, Inc., 1976)

Staying Together: Marriages That Work by Patricia O'Brien (Pocket Books, 1978)

A Strategy for Success by Dr. Ari Kiev (Macmillan, 1977)

Try Marriage Before Divorce by James E. Kilgore (Word Books, 1978)

One of the best ways of getting to know another person is to get to know yourself. Among the many books on this topic:

Being and Caring by Victor Daniels (Mayfield Publishers, 1976)

Dr. Rubin, Please Make Me Happy by Theodore Isaac Rubin (Arbor House, 1974)

Finding Yourself, Finding Others by Clark E. Moustakas (Prentice-Hall, 1975)

How to Be Your Own Best Friend by Mildred Newman (Random House, 1973)

How to Live 365 Days a Year by John A. Schindler (Parker/Prentice-Hall, 1954)

I'm OK—You're OK by Thomas A. Harris (Harper & Row, 1969)

Norman Vincent Peale's books:

The Power of Positive Thinking (Fawcett/Crest, 1978)

Guide to Confident Living (Fawcett/Crest, 1977)

You Can If You Think You Can (Fawcett/Crest, 1978)

Enthusiasm Makes the Difference (Fawcett/Crest, 1978)

The Psychology Today Omnibook of Personal Development by Katinka Matson (Morrow, 1977)

Successful Living Day by Day by Nelson Boswell (Fawcett/Crest, 1977)

Your Erroneous Zones by Wayne Dyer (T.Y. Crowell, 1976)

The You That Could Be by Fitzhugh Dodson (Follett, 1976; in paperback, Pocket Books/Simon & Schuster, 1977)

W O R K S H O P S

Couple Communication
300 Clifton Ave.
At the Carriage House
Minneapolis, MN 55403
(Provides information on courses offered throughout the country.)

Marital Workshops, Inc.
P.O. Box 597
Merrick, NY 11566

REAL Program
West Los Angeles–Beverly Hills YWCA
10936 Santa Monica Blvd.
Los Angeles, CA 90025
(A special program to teach teenagers about life's realities.)

B O O K S   O N   M E N T A L   H E A L T H

A Complete Guide to Therapy by Joel Kovel, M.D. (Pantheon, 1976)

Consumer's Guide to Mental Health by Brian L. Mishara and Robert Patterson (Time Books, 1977)

HELP: A Guide to Counseling and Therapy Without a Hassle by Jane Marks (Julian Messner/Simon & Schuster, 1976)

How to Get Your Money's Worth Out of Psychiatry by Herbert R. Lazarus (Sherbourne, 1978)

Mental Health Directory (Supt. of Documents, U.S. Government Printing Office, Washington, DC 20402)

Shrinks, Etc. by Thomas Kiernan (Dial Press, 1974; in paperback, Dell, 1976)

OTHER RESOURCES

Many universities and churches conduct special programs on marriage; inquire about those held in your community.

Dr. Marvin B. Sussman
Institute of the Family and the Bureaucratic Society
Haydn Hall
Case Western Reserve University
Cleveland, OH 44106
(Information and advice on personal marriage contracts.)

THE SECOND TIME AROUND

The Divorce Experience: A New Look at the World of the Formerly Married by Bernice and Morton Hunt (McGraw-Hill, 1979; in paperback, NAL, 1979)
Learning to Love Again by Mel Krantzler (T.Y. Crowell, 1977)

The Food of Love

For suggestions about different types of foods you might want to try, read the food columns in your local newspaper and in travel magazines; subscribe to a gourmet food magazine; scan recipes in international cookbooks; ask your favorite waiter to describe unknown dishes (but only when business is slow). Be adventurous: order one dish that you know and one that you don't, then split them between you.

BOOKS

Aphrodisiacs: From Legend to Prescription by Alan Hull Walton (Associated Booksellers, 1958)
The Complete Food Catalogue by Jose Wilson (Holt, Rinehart & Winston)
Cook's and Diner's Dictionary (Funk & Wagnall's)
A Dictionary of Gastronomy by Robin Howe and Andre Louis Simon (Overlook Press, 1979)

Don't Ask Your Waiter by Pauline and Sheldon Wasserman (Stein & Day, 1979)

Eating in Eight Languages by Wilma George (Stein & Day, 1974)

The Encyclopedia of Food by Artemas Ward (Peter Smith, 6 Lexington Ave., Magnolia, MA 01930)

Food and Menu Dictionary by Grete M. Dahl (CBI Publishing Co., 51 Sleeper St., Boston, MA 02210)

The Food of France by Waverly Root (Alfred Knopf, 1958)

Food Power by George Schwartz, M.D. (McGraw-Hill, 1979)

Lewd Food by Robert Hendrickson (Chilton, 1974)

Marling Menu-Master (Rough and Ready, CA 95975). Booklets for France, Germany, Mexico, Spain.

Social Skills and Conversational Arts

BOOKS

Asserting Yourself by Gordon and Sharon Bower (Addison-Wesley, 1976)

Breaking Through to Each Other by Dr. Jesse S. Nirenberg (Harper & Row, 1976)

How to Put Yourself Across With Key Words and Phrases by Martha W. Cresci (Prentice-Hall, 1973)

How to Talk With Practically Anybody About Practically Anything by Barbara Walters (Dell, 1971)

Making Contact by Arthur C. Wassmer, Ph.D. (Dial, 1978)

The Shy Person's Book by Claire Rayner (Barnes & Noble Books/ Harper & Row, 1976)

Shyness: What It Is, What to Do About It by Philip Zimbardo (Addison-Wesley, 1977)

What Do You Say After You Say Hello? by Eric Berne (Bantam, 1975)

Etiquette

BOOKS

Charlotte Ford's Book of Modern Manners by Charlotte Ford (Simon and Schuster, 1980)

The Amy Vanderbilt Complete Book of Etiquette: A Guide to Contemporary Living revised and expanded by Letitia Baldridge (Doubleday, 1978)

The New Emily Post's Etiquette by Emily Post (Crowell, 1975)

The Mirror of Your Image

BOOKS / BOOKLETS

The Aida Grey Beauty Book by Aida Grey (Lippincott & Crowell, 1979)

The AMA Book of Skin and Hair Care by Linda Allen Schoen (Lippincott, 1976)

Be Beautiful by Celia Haddon (Summit Books, 1979)

Beauty Through Health by Lawrence M. Steinhart (Arbor House, 1974)

The Black Is Beautiful Beauty Book by Melba Miller (Prentice-Hall, 1975)

The Complete Herbal Guide to Natural Health and Beauty by Dian Dincin Buchman (Doubleday, 1973)

Diane von Furstenberg's Book of Beauty by Diane von Furstenberg (Simon & Schuster, 1977)

The Easy Way to Good Looks by Shirley Lord (Crowell, 1976)

Eileen Ford's Beauty Now and Forever by Eileen Ford (Simon & Schuster, 1977)

The Foot Book by Harry F. Hlavac (World Publications, 1977)

Glamour's Health and Beauty Book by Glamour Editors (Simon & Schuster, 1978)

The Herbal Guide to Inner Beauty by Jeanne Rose (Grosset & Dunlap, 1978)

Looking Good by Charles Hix (Hawthorn Books, 1978)

The Medically Based No-Nonsense Beauty Book by Deborah Chase (Knopf, 1974; in paperback, Pocket Books, 1976)

The Models' Way to Beauty, Slenderness and Glowing Health by Oleda Baker and Bill Gale (Ballantine, 1976)

The Natural Way to Super Beauty by Mary Ann Crenshaw (Dell, 1975)

The New You by Wilhelmina (Simon & Schuster, 1978)

The Sally Struthers Natural Beauty Book by Sally Struthers and Joyce Virtue, with Jane Wilkie (Doubleday, 1979)

Totally Natural Beauty by Non Aguilar (Rawson, 1977)

Vogue Body and Beauty Book by Meredith Bronwen (Harper & Row, 1979)

Your Health and Your Hair by Paul Chappius Bragg (Health Science, P.O. Box 7, Santa Barbara, CA 96102)

Educational Booklets
Consumer Satisfaction Dept.
Clairol
345 Park Ave.
New York, NY 10022
(You can also call Clairol Hotline with a question about your hair or any Clairol product. The number is 212–644–2990; call weekdays between 9 and 5 EDT. Outside of New York, call 1–800–223–5800.)

Coppertone Tanning Guide
Plough, Inc.
Memphis, TN 38151

The History, the Mystery, the Enjoyment of Fragrance
The Fragrance Association
110 E. 19th St.
New York, NY 10003

Metamorphosis
The Butterfly Group
World of Beauty
623 S. Wabash Ave.
Chicago, IL 60605
(Booklets on skin care and make-up.)

New Foot Book
Scholl, Inc.
Room 801
150 E. Huron St.
Chicago, IL 60611

The Sun and Your Skin
Order Dept.
American Medical Association
535 N. Dearborn St.
Chicago, IL 60610

Sun Leaflet
Public Relations Dept.
Johnson & Johnson
New Brunswick, NJ 08903

You're Beautiful
Johnson & Johnson Baby Products Co.
New Brunswick, NJ 08903
(On skin and hair care for teens.)

Your Skin and the Sun
Eclipse Sun Booklet
2525 Dupont Drive
Irvine, CA 92713

TIP

If you suffer an adverse effect from any cosmetic, notify the manufacturer immediately. Also notify:

Food and Drug Administration
Division of Cosmetics Technology
HFF-430
200 C St., NW
Washington, DC 20204

INDEX